#NoFilter

"I first heard Jodi speak at a Thanksgiving banquet, and I knew immediately I needed her to be our keynote speaker at a Women's 20/20 Vision event. Because of Covid, the event was never held, and we never got to hear what God had placed on her heart about vision. *#NoFilter* was well worth the wait, and I'm thrilled to see how God worked through Jodi's heart to expand on this topic by peeling back our visual filters. Women can now sit down with this study and dig deep into God's Word. As a speaker and writer, Jodi is one of the most passionate, transparent women I know with a true desire to love and serve Jesus by sharing her heart with others."

Rose Alexa
Women's Ministry Leader
Central Baptist Association of New Mexico

"Many are allowing life experiences, circumstances, and the past to create their identity. *#NoFilter* helps us to get a God-lens and proper view on who we truly are. The connection that Jodi makes with God's Word and life is helpful to unburden us from the expectations we set in our lives. I was helped and challenged—and enjoyed some laughter as well. This devotional is such a practical help to not just women, but a help to me as a man and pastor."

Justin Burkholder
Pastor
Liberty Baptist Church, CA

"In a culture that seems to intentionally distort our vision, *#NoFilter* is a relevant and timely study that will benefit any Christian. Jodi does a beautiful job weaving in commentary and life experiences to the Scripture-focused text. I highly recommend it to anyone who wants a clearer view of themselves and their Creator."

Amanda Banks
Vice President
Family Policy Foundation

"Christian women of all ages deserve to have deeper biblical content and not simply reheated leftovers from pop psychology. I'm excited to recommend *#NoFilter* to any of my sisters-in-Christ!"

Ben Everson
International Evangelist

"Jodi is a creative and gifted communicator. She brings life from the Scripture to everyday living. This is a must-read for women who desire to find God's purpose and meaning in their faith journey. Jodi lives out her faith in her ministry to women with passion and excellence. You will discover biblical principles that will strengthen and transform your relationship with Christ."

Derek Witt
Lead Pastor
Metamorphi Church, New Mexico

"You will find yourself digging into God's Word with Jodi's *#NoFilter* book as she guides you through a place to reflect and challenge you to see how to discover God's plan for us."

Paula Gonzales
Executive Director
CareNet ABQ

"In her book, Jodi challenges readers with real-life situations, rather than just providing a typical feel-good "God loves you no matter what" devotional. She delves into the stories of biblical characters, exploring their pasts and the incredible transformations they experienced after surrendering to God. The chance to study Scripture and then reflect on our own lives using the Word is truly refreshing."

Representative Rebecca Dow
NM House of Representatives

#NoFilter

UNMASKING THE WOMAN GOD CREATED YOU TO BE

Jodi Hendricks

AMBASSADOR INTERNATIONAL
GREENVILLE, SOUTH CAROLINA & BELFAST, NORTHERN IRELAND
www.ambassador-international.com

#NoFilter

Unmasking the Woman God Created You to Be
Hashtag series, Book 1
©2024 by Jodi Hendricks
All rights reserved

ISBN: 978-1-64960-129-2, hardcover
ISBN: 978-1-64960-695-2, paperback
eISBN: 978-1-64960-179-7

Cover Design by Hannah Linder Designs
Interior Typesetting by Dentelle Design
Edited by Kimberly Davis
Author photo by Lavel Marie Nordin with Lavel Marie Photography

Unless otherwise noted, Scripture taken from the New American Standard Bible®, Copyright © 1960, 1971, 1977, 1995 by The Lockman Foundation. All rights reserved.

Scripture also taken from the Holy Bible, New Living Translation, copyright © 1996, 2004, 2015 by Tyndale House Foundation. Used by permission of Tyndale House Publishers, Inc., Carol Stream, Illinois 60188. All rights reserved.

Ambassador International titles may be purchased in bulk for education, business, fundraising, or sales promotional use. For information, please email sales@emeraldhouse.com.

AMBASSADOR INTERNATIONAL
Emerald House
411 University Ridge, Suite B14
Greenville, SC 29601
United States
www.ambassador-international.com

AMBASSADOR BOOKS
The Mount
2 Woodstock Link
Belfast, BT6 8DD
Northern Ireland, United Kingdom
www.ambassadormedia.co.uk

The colophon is a trademark of Ambassador, a Christian publishing company.

To my husband, Michael, who never fails to put a smile on my face and remind me that I need no filters.

To my children, Isabella, Tristen, Lilly and Addyson—may you grow in the confidence of who God made you to be and walk in the truth that, as creations of the Creator Himself, you need no filter.

TABLE OF CONTENTS

FOREWORD

I'm Ben Everson, an itinerant musician and evangelist, ministering to thousands of people each year. I've known Jodi Hendricks for almost twenty years. She and I are alike in that we married into the same family. I know firsthand her qualifications, both personal and professional, to write a book like this.

I meet many people all the time, and I'm constantly being asked about resources. My heart is thrilled to have a resource like this book you hold in your hands. We have a lot of content being pushed on us, and one would think we have more than we could ever ask for. In particular, the resource list for women looks long. But when you begin to weed out the fluff, the emotionally manipulative, and the self-help books masquerading as biblical help books, you begin to see a real need.

I have benefitted much from godly women. Like Timothy with his mother and grandmother, I learned from my Sunday School teachers, my mother, and—since I went to an excellent Christian school—many of my schoolteachers. My wife is the most important person in my life, and we learn from each other on a consistent basis as we follow our Lord together. I love to see the rare resource that takes women seriously as equal creations of God, whose souls the Lord values just as much as their male counterparts.

This book, *#NoFilter*, takes the need for biblically sound encouragement for women seriously. I was cringing when I downloaded the proof copy, wondering if I was going to encounter the sugary "you are enough" pablum

1

that runs rampant. Not only was I relieved, then surprised, but I also benefited. We have so many lenses through which we see our lives. In most cases, we're subconsciously doing this; and it distorts our perspective on ourselves, those we love, and God Himself. Jodi carefully and honestly shows us these lenses and contrasts them with what the Word of God says. It leads us to consider and then to change.

I say *us* because I'm not ashamed to admit I was challenged by what I read. I unreservedly recommend this book to you, the reader, and any of the women in your life. I'll be recommending it to those in mine.

And if you leave it lying around, anyone can benefit from reading because it is firstly a biblical study. This book takes women seriously because it takes the Bible seriously. It's a relatable read because Jodi integrates real life with real Scripture, instead of just sprinkling verses to qualify it as a "Christian" study. How refreshing!

Ben Everson

International Evangelist

AUTHOR'S NOTE

The fact that you have this book in your hands brings me joy. It is my prayer that, as you read these pages, you see yourself as the Creator sees you—a beautiful masterpiece. It took many years for me to realize how filters distorted my vision, both of myself and of God.

I'm so incredibly thankful that my Heavenly Father took me on the journey of exposing the filters and allowed me to discover truth. As each filter was peeled away and rejected, something inside me was unleashed; and I was invited to step confidently into who I was created to be—not as the world saw me but as the Creator Himself had always intended me to be.

Do filters still creep in from time to time? Of course. But now that I know what they look like, I'm better equipped to call them what they are and strip them away. Beautiful one, you are a masterpiece. You need no filter. Now get ready to unleash who you were created to be!

INTRODUCTION

Have you ever had a moment when everything you have been waiting on God to do seems to fall into place, just as you imagined it would; but then you quickly begin to see that it was not how you imagined at all? Before you know it, you have embarked on a path that challenges everything you thought you knew and everything you thought you were prepared for.

This kind of journey can be life-changing, and I invite you to join me. The filters through which your vision has been established will be stripped away to reveal something that exceeds anything you could ask or think. In fact, filters you did not even realize you use are revealed for the distortion they cause and replaced with the truth God desires to instill in your heart and mind—who you are, what you were made for, and what God has given you to achieve your purpose in this life.

My own life-changing journey began several years ago when I received a call from a ministry, asking me to speak at an upcoming women's event in our area. As a girl who loves any opportunity to talk, my heart fluttered at the idea. Before screaming "YES!" at the sweet woman on the other end of the phone, I took a breath, told those butterflies to settle down, and asked the Lord for wisdom and guidance.

We talked about the director's hopes, and she shared that the one word on her heart for the conference was *vision*—fitting, as the conference was to be held in 2020, and the concept was having 20/20 vision in 2020. Since the mere mention of the year 2020 probably makes you cringe, I assure you that God used it to show me just how skewed my vision really was.

On the phone, I could not help but smile. It was right there—God's overwhelming and comforting hand in my life, nudging me once again. But I get ahead of myself.

About three months earlier, I was going through a process that I believed was meant to lead me one step closer to my dream job. It ended up being a complete disappointment and brought me to my knees before the Lord in discouragement and, well, sadness. I did not understand why the Lord brought me so close to something I desired so much, only to yank it away without a word as to why or with a new direction in its place.

As I fought through this frustration, friends and acquaintances around me started talking about picking their "word" for the coming year. You know how that goes; you pick a word that you believe is something the Lord will build or refine in you, and it becomes your theme for the upcoming year. I had never done this, far less taken the time to consider it, and I had never really put much stock in it. Sure, I saw it make a difference in a few people's lives over the years, but most people I knew forgot about their word by January 2! Or they no longer talked about it as a theme for their year. But now, in my heartsickness, I felt a desperate need for guidance. Maybe, just maybe, the Lord was trying to show me something that I needed to be willing to see. I began considering a word for my upcoming year.

I spent time, thought, and prayer in choosing it. After all, I did not want to choose something silly, like patience. I have four kids; the Lord already has plenty of avenues to teach that, and I do not need to ask for it. I kept trying to think of something that went with the theme I already saw in my life over the past several years. My own heart, family, and marriage had experienced restoration and healing; and I had gained such a new sense of purpose that I felt like my word should fit with what I already saw God do.

One morning in my devotion time, the Lord led me to Isaiah 43:18: "Do not call to mind the former things, Or ponder things of the past." Ouch! My entire premise of looking for the word emphasized remembering the past. Yet here was the idea, clear as day, that I was looking in the wrong place. In this passage of Scripture, God reminds Israel of great miracles He worked on their behalf before bringing them to the present and telling them that no matter what He brought them through, their focus was to be fixed forward.

The Lord had helped my family overcome so much; but while I can draw strength and encouragement, it is not the place He wants me to concentrate. I continued to read in Isaiah 43, "Behold, I will do something new, Now it will spring forth; Will you not be aware of it? I will even make a roadway in the wilderness, Rivers in the desert" (v. 19). At that moment, I recognized my word: *new.*

Initially, I thought a new career path was still on the horizon, and I needed only to wait for it. Who would not want to see roadways through the wilderness and rivers in the desert? From my limited perspective, I saw only disappointment in what I had decided was the right path, but God knew I needed a big, flashing neon sign to catch on to what He wanted to get through to me. God had something else in mind.

Over the first three months of 2019, before receiving the phone call, the Lord began to show me that *new* meant something far greater—something my minimal understanding was not quite ready to fathom. He was definitely doing something new in me; I was in desperate need of a life-changing shift in my vision to *see* what He was doing. I needed *vision.*

That April, I tried not to shout in excitement at the poor woman on the phone. In that single conversation with someone who did not know my heart's desires nor what work the Lord had already begun in me, I was reminded that He truly does have a purpose. He sees the bigger picture, and I must allow Him to change my vision, in order to experience His blessing fully. I accepted the invitation to speak at the event and eagerly set on a path to discover both the *new vision* God wanted me to have and how I could encourage other women in the same process.

Today I can attest that God changed my vision in ways I never expected, dreamed of, or even hoped for; and it is a process that continues daily. I pray that sharing how God changed my vision will be a blessing and encouragement—and a challenge to allow Him access to the inner recesses of the heart and mind, to shatter the lenses created through lies, to remove filters that distort understanding, and to enlighten the heart's eye to see with a vision that is formed, refined, and sharpened by God: no lies, no filters, just God's intended point of view.

Week 1

Day 1

JUST ASK

My youngest daughter is notorious for beating around the bush when she wants something. If I am eating a snack that she would also like, she sits next to me on the couch and says, "That looks really yummy, Mommy." She proceeds to bat her eyelashes and looks from me to the snack. If I do not offer to share, her nonchalant attempt continues. "I never get to have snacks like that," she sighs, boring her eyes into my soul and waiting for me to extend an invitation to share. She keeps up her indirect comments and eyelash batting, sometimes even cozying in close and laying her head on my shoulder. She wants something, but she has not come out and said so.

After a while, I say, "Oh, did you want some, baby?" Victorious, she nods emphatically, to which I respond, "All you had to do was ask."

As we begin this journey to life-changing vision, we must start with the basic necessity of simply asking for it. It is time to stop beating around the bush with insecurity over the answer. Do you want to destroy unintended filters in your vision? Do you want to see with the vision God intended for you? All you must do is ask.

Maybe you are cozied up to the Father, like my daughter does to me, and are ready to finally blurt out your desire for this new vision. I am excited for your enthusiasm! Perhaps we have some stragglers in the back. You began this study because you liked the cover, or a phrase caught your attention, or a friend dragged you into it—but you are not really sure what it is all about. Maybe you are a bit hesitant to jump on board with this life-changing shift. I get it. Things are comfortable right now, and you are afraid to give that up. The thought of removing some blinders terrifies you. Whatever it may be, I understand.

The crazy thing about this journey is that you have no idea what lies in store for you. Because it involves drawing closer to the Heavenly Father, I guarantee it will be for your good. Now, what exactly do we mean by *vision*, and why is it so important? I am glad you asked.

The concept of our vision (what we see with spiritually enlightened eyes) and understanding *what* we see are vital pieces—not only to the bigger picture that involves our purpose but also to our vision of the small things and of ourselves. If we continue navigating through life with a distorted view of where we are going, where we have been, or even who we are, then we have fallen victim to the limitations of our own understanding. Since Scripture admonishes us *not* to rely on our own understanding, it is clear that we desperately need to grow in our knowledge of God so our spiritual wisdom and insight can grow and allow us to trust the Father with all of our heart.

My prayer for you, as you step away from your own understanding, is what Paul prayed for the Ephesians—"that the God of our Lord Jesus Christ, the Father of glory, may give to you a spirit of wisdom and of revelation in the knowledge of Him" (Eph. 1:17).

Consider the Context

READ EPHESIANS 1.

Paul begins his letter by reminding the Ephesians of all that God has done for them. List those things here._____

_____

_____

_____

Paul praises God that the Ephesians heard and believed what He did for them. For this reason, he offers his prayer, saturated with purpose and power. The "spirit of wisdom" he asks for is one that actively develops infinite wisdom in believers. It is not a limited, worldly wisdom but an infinite spiritual discernment that is worked, refined, and grown in us who believe.

This spiritual insight matures as our relationship with God grows deeper. Spiritual mysteries are revealed to believers as they grow in their knowledge of God. I often consider my own purpose and God's plan for my life to be a mystery, not unlike many other spiritual mysteries interwoven in our faith. The acumen necessary to recognize and comprehend these mysteries is available to the believer; all we must do is ask. Are you willing to ask? Are you tired of trying to function within your own capacity of understanding and imperfect vision?

Spiritual wisdom is continually and actively growing us in our knowledge of God.

Dig a little Deeper

What do the following verses tell you about "asking?"

Matthew 21:22 _____

_____

James 4:3 _____

_____

John 16:24 _____

_____

I John 3:22 _____

_____

Where are my stragglers? You might be afraid to ask for this new vision because, deep down, you are terrified of what God might show you. Today is the day to let go of fear. Do not let fear hold you back from experiencing the hope to which our glorious Lord has called you. This life might very well be terrifying. Past experiences may have left you wounded and in desperate need of healing.

Trust me, I have been there. I have felt the soul-deep emptiness of loss, heartbreak, and fear. It still occasionally rears its ugly head, often when I least expect it. But my sweet Lord gently speaks to my heart and tells me, "Do not fear, for I am with you; Do not anxiously look about you, for I am your God. I will strengthen you, surely I will help you, Surely I will uphold you with My righteous right hand" (Isa. 41:10).

Do not give in to this spirit of fear. Claim as your own the promise of "power and love and discipline" (2 Tim. 1:7). Allow the eyes of your heart to be enlightened. Let light pass through the lens of your vision to reveal Life; for where there is light, there is life (John 1:4).

Are you ready? Let's do this!

Refining Reflection

READ PROVERBS 3:5-7.

In what ways do you "lean on your own understanding" (v. 5)?_____

_____

_____

In what areas is it difficult to trust the Lord rather than your own understanding?

_____

_____

What would it look like for you to acknowledge Him in all your ways (v. 6)?

_____

_____

_____

_____

Proverbs 3:8 tells us, "It will be healing to your body And refreshment to your bones." Like a tall glass of water on a hot day, trusting the Lord with our vision brings healing and refreshment to our souls that satisfies and electrifies us. It wakes us every day with excitement to see what our Father has in store. Are you ready for that kind of healing? It is time to remove the filters.

Additional Notes

_____

_____

_____

_____

_____

_____

_____

# #

Day 2

WHO IS THIS PAUL?

A testimony is a powerful thing. Simply stated, a person's words weigh more significantly when you know her story. For example, many of you have experienced loss, maybe even the devastating loss of a miscarriage, which is confusing and tears you apart from the inside. Well-meaning people may try to console you with sweet thoughts about your baby's being in heaven. They might even suggest thoughts like, "At least you weren't too far along," or some such nonsense that invalidates your pain and leaves you feeling even more broken and inadequate.

If you have ever suffered a miscarriage, you know what I am talking about. People's best intentions of comfort end up causing even more pain, as you discover they have no idea what you truly feel. The comfort these well-wishers attempt to provide falls flat.

What if I were to offer compassion by sitting beside you as you feel all the brokenness, outrage, and devastation? I share that I have been where you are and know well the soul-deep ache—not to compare grief but to show you that I truly understand. As we sit together, my words may begin to have a greater effect because you know I do not offer shallow platitudes that have no value. They move you differently because you become aware that I *have* been where you are, and my story also involves the healing that, in this moment, you fear may never come.

You may not be ready to hear that. You may not be ready to let go of the anger or the hurt; you need to grieve. But my words will be filed away, drawn to the surface later when you need them, rather than tossed in the trash as unfeeling and meaningless. Your perspective on my words changes as my testimony is revealed.

It would be a great disservice to our study if we fail to consider the testimony of the man who offered this beautiful prayer of wisdom, insight, and vision. As we pull together pieces of Paul's story, our connection to him brings greater connection to the message he delivers.

Consider the Context

Paul begins his prayer for the church in Ephesus by making absolutely clear that it is the Father above, the one and only God, Who can impart wisdom and insight to the people. Read his greeting to the Ephesians and his prayer for them before we dive into Paul's story.

READ EPHESIANS 1 AGAIN.

In verses 1-14 and 19b-23, what key characteristics of God does Paul bring to our attention? _____

_____

_____

Consider the prayer.

> I do not cease giving thanks for you, while making mention of you in my prayers; that the God of our Lord Jesus Christ, the Father of glory, may give to you *a spirit of wisdom and of revelation in the knowledge of Him.* I pray that *the eyes of your heart may be enlightened,* so that you will know what is *the hope of His calling,* what are *the riches of the glory of His inheritance*

in the saints, and what is the *surpassing greatness of His power toward us who believe* (Eph. 1:16-19a).

Put into your own words what Paul desires for the believer. Do not worry about coming up with the perfect answer; we will dig further into this idea. Taking time to meditate on it for yourself helps your understanding grow as we move along. _____

_____

_____

_____

_____

The concept of vision was real to Paul; knowing his story helps us understand more deeply his desire for the believer. His story is one of remarkable transformation that showcases the harsh reality of an unpleasant past and the astonishing grace of God as something new and steadfast emerges.

READ ACTS 7:57-60.

We have stepped right into the gruesome stoning of Stephen, a man full of God's grace and power. He performed amazing miracles and signs among the people; and when God is on the move, you can guarantee opposition.

Stephen's opposition came as men decided to lie about him, saying he blasphemed against God. He was arrested, a slew of accusations hurled against him. His response turned into an accusation of his own as he laid out the Gospel message of Jesus and accused the Jewish leaders of betraying and murdering the Messiah and deliberately disobeying God's law. You can imagine how the men received his words. As the scene unfolds, we find them full of rage, dragging Stephen out of the city and stoning him. Amid this horrifying series of events, we meet Saul.

Dig a little Deeper

What role does Saul play in the events of Stephen's stoning? _____

_____

_____

_____

_____

What does Saul's role reveal to us about Saul and his position regarding the Gospel of Jesus? _____

_____

_____

_____

_____

This brief introduction to Saul reveals his part in the dark deed. The fact that he was close enough to hold the clothing of the men who stoned Stephen reveals the depth of his involvement. As a young man, he was already part of the Sanhedrin, the supreme council in charge of Jewish affairs in Rome. His place at the stoning of Stephen was not coincidental but intentional—a hearty agreement with the proceedings that reveals his ruthless hatred for all believers.

READ ACTS 8:1-4.

In just a few short verses, Saul takes center stage as the driving force for the great persecution of the Church. This oppression scattered the people beyond Jerusalem and resulted in imprisoning many believers for their faith. At this point, Saul resembles a character similar to the Sheriff of Nottingham in the story of Robin Hood; the difference, unfortunately, is that Saul is not fictional. Hatred for followers of Jesus fueled his villainous ways, and he stopped at nothing to see the Church destroyed. "But Saul began ravaging the church, entering house after house, and dragging off men and women, he would put them in prison" (Acts 8:3).

I want you to have a clear picture of the depth of Saul's campaign—the term *ravaging* should paint a pretty gruesome picture in your mind. It means to cause harm to, injure, or damage. To understand it further in context, imagine something that has been mangled by a wild animal; now you understand Saul's mission regarding the Church and all believers. He was a man led by seething hatred. It saturated his heart, consumed his thoughts, and drove his actions. Saul was dangerous. His every breath threatened people who believed that Jesus was the Messiah. He believed his murderous hatred was justified, and he was on a mission to see the Church snuffed out of existence.

The past can be an ugly thing. We all have a story that is told in perspective of past and present—where we came from versus where we are now. Stories reflect how young or foolish we were then in contrast with maturity gained over time. Some tales show feats of accomplishment, like achieving weight loss or preparing for a marathon, that started in a place you had to move from in order to see the transformation you desired.

All stories feature a metamorphosis from something old to something new or the desire to see such a change. No matter the story, we must reflect on where we were, so we can put into perspective where we are now. Saul was in a dark place. But the horrible things he did and countless lives he ruined are merely the past portion of his story; the future that awaited was nothing short of miraculous.

Refining Reflection

READ ACTS 8:3 AGAIN.

What is your opinion of Saul in the midst of the past portion of his story? __

_____

_____

_____

_____

Reflect on your own transformation—the part of your story that showcases where you came from. No matter where you are today, I know it is not your final stopping place. However, in order to value where we are and where we are going even more, we must reflect on where we have been (or possibly where we feel we still are).

Where have you come from? _____

_____

_____

_____

_____

_____

Many of us look back on where we have been and cringe. *If only I had known . . . If only I had been . . . If only I had . . .* Maybe you can identify with Saul's past, having participated in something that horrifies you today, or maybe your story seems boring, in light of Saul's. Maybe you were spared from being the driving force of something, and you find yourself a bit more reflective on things done to you and your responses to them. Either way, these things in our past shape our identity and filter our vision. It is time to begin scrubbing away the filter.

How has your past affected the way you see yourself today? I am not looking for the Sunday school answer. Be real with yourself. Do you feel valuable? Do you feel lovable? Do you feel confident? Do you feel shame? Do you have a hard time accepting that you are included when the Lord says, "You are precious in My sight . . . you are honored and I love you" (Isa. 43:4).

This verse gives us a glimpse of God's heart toward His redeemed nation, Israel. We, as His redeemed people, have been accepted in the beloved; we can find hope and comfort in the fact that He looks at us with the same thoughts: precious, honored, and loved.

If you could label the filters that your past lays over your vision of yourself, what would those labels be? (i.e., unforgivable, unlovable, ugly, weak, worthless) _____

_____

_____

_____

You were never meant to bear such filters; it is time to let them go. Take your first step in faith by choosing to believe you are who *God* says you are—not who you fear your past has determined you to be.

As we close today, journal a prayer that surrenders these filters to the Lord.

_____

_____

Day 3

TRANSFORMATION

Yesterday, we left Saul in the heat of his ravaging campaign against the Church. Our opinion of this man, if we did not already know the outcome of his story, is not a good one. He drags men and women from their homes, throws them in prison, and breathes threats of murder against the disciples. The next passage shows Saul, continuing his murderous campaign.

READ ACTS 9:1-2.

Saul is so zealous in his efforts that his ambition extends beyond Jerusalem. He requests that the high priest in Jerusalem write letters to the synagogues in Damascus, granting permission to continue annihilating the Church. Damascus, located northeast of Jerusalem, is home to a large population of Jews, many of whom fled Jerusalem to escape Saul's persecution. On his way to Damascus, though, God intervenes, changing not only Saul's path but also his vision.

READ ACTS 9:3-9.

Imagine the reality of this moment. Saul walks down the road on a mission of destruction. Without warning, his vision floods with the pure Presence of unfiltered, heavenly light. Talk about getting his attention! This flash of Divine glory stops Saul in his tracks, brings him to his knees, and forever alters the course of his life. God uses this unfiltered experience to reveal Himself and to remove Saul's filters of justification and self-righteousness that galvanized his brutality. In that moment, Saul experiences the unfiltered truth that Jesus is God, and Saul had been wrong.

Saul's conversion account begins with his seeing a light from Heaven flash around him and ends with his having no sight at all. I like to think that the Lord wanted that heavenly light to be seared into Saul's mind and heart, denying any other physical vision to distract or interfere. Whatever the reason, Saul does not regain his sight for three days.

Think about that. For God to change the vision of this man, who issued threats and committed murder, He chooses to remove the motivating force of *Saul's* vision, which had been limited to his own understanding as a Pharisee. Saul had seen what was in front of him through his own filters and determined for himself what needed to be done.

By the time God returns his physical sense of sight, his vision is forever changed. Saul sees himself, absent his illegitimate filters and in light of God's glorious grace. He sees the little things around him through the reality of God's presence, and he begins to notice a more aerial view of the bigger picture through the hope of God's power and might. The pharisaical, human, sin-tainted filters removed, Saul emerges, a new creation with no filters.

Consider the Context

READ ACTS 9:10-22.

As the scales fell from his eyes, Saul *regained* physical vision and *gained* new spiritual vision. Consider how Saul's life and mission changed in the dawn of this new vision. _____

_____

_____

Where once Saul used the tip of persecution's spear against the Gospel of Jesus, how quickly did he step into his role in the unfiltered vision that God gave him? (See Gal. 1:16-18.) _____

_____

_____

_____

His new role in this unfiltered vision begins immediately because he allows his mind and heart to be transformed. Saul does not waste time, wallowing in regret and shame. That said, his public ministry does not begin right away. He trains for three years in other regions before returning to Jerusalem. His new vision brings a sense of urgency, as well as an acceptance of the forgiveness Christ offers when we come to Him with a repentant heart.

Saul knows that time is needed to prepare his heart and mind before embarking on public ministry. He does not step into his usual leadership role the second after his conversion; rather, his ministry ties closely to that of the disciples in those early days. His preaching the Gospel in Jerusalem causes an uproar, and plots of murder form against him.

The disciples send him to Tarsus, where eventually Barnabas finds him and brings him to work with the church in Antioch. Here, Barnabas leads as the main speaker and decision-maker, and Saul takes a back seat (not something he was used to). As he gains experience and grows in this new vision, a shift comes in Acts 13; Saul becomes Paul.

No grand moment is called out when the change officially comes; in fact, the name *Saul* versus *Paul* is actually just the difference between the Hebrew and Roman. However, a shift occurs, nonetheless, and the timing is beautiful. *Saul* struck fear in the hearts of Jewish believers yet was appropriate within pharisaical circles. On the other hand, *Paul* was more accepted and recognized within Gentile culture—interesting, in light of where God leads Paul.

Dig a little Deeper

In Acts 13, Saul and Barnabas travel to Paphos. They face an interfering false prophet who urges the governor to pay no attention to their message. At this point, Saul takes the lead, instead of Barnabas; and Luke, the author of Acts—as well as a disciple, friend, travel companion, and personal physician to Saul—purposely shifts the narrative to put away the name tied to Saul's past. This decision presents him in the light of his new vision, which was beginning to transform.

READ ACTS 13:6-12.

Based on the account of Paul's actions in this passage, how do you believe his vision is transforming in terms of people, of himself, and of God? _____

_____

_____

_____

_____

After this shift in leadership, in Acts 14, Paul tries one last time to preach to the Jews in the synagogue, only to see them reject the Gospel once again. It is at this time in history that God directs Paul to become the first missionary to take the Gospel to the Gentiles. He goes from Saul, the Pharisee, to Paul, the missionary—a transformation only God could achieve.

When unintended filters are removed, we gain the blessed freedom to step into our God-given purpose. This cleared vision holds no space for shame, regret, or worthlessness because, in this unfiltered space, you view yourself as the creation God intended you to be. You see that God continually equips you with the tools necessary to fulfill His calling on your life.

God did not make a mistake in His plan for you. He has kept an unfiltered vision for and of you from the beginning. During ongoing battle in the spiritual realm, sin slithered in and dropped filter after filter over our vision; and they kill, steal, and destroy us from the inside out. What the enemy did not consider, though, is that he may have meant it for evil, but "God meant it for good" (Gen. 50:20).

In the same way, what Saul may have meant for evil in his humanly filtered vision, God used to accomplish His purpose.

READ ACTS 8:4.

What good came from the evil of Saul's annihilation campaign? _____

_____

_____

_____

_____

Did you catch the fact that while Saul's persecution and ravaging was going on, believers scattered? As they moved about geographically, they took the Gospel with them. Saul's attempt to dismantle the Church actually spread the Gospel to places believers might otherwise not have gone. He was, unaware, responsible for the first-ever missionary outreach of the Church. Tell me that does not give you goosebumps. We can clearly see a horrible and devastating past turned into something God used for His glory.

Do we experience shame and heartache over past decisions? Yes! We must come to repentance and experience transformation, but we cannot live there. God was at work long before we entered the picture. He knew the mistakes we would make and the enemy traps that lay in wait; in His unfailing love, He shows His power over our past and brings beauty from the ashes.

A changed man, Paul does not wallow in regret. He chooses to live out God's purpose for him, unencumbered by the filters of other people's opinions, unhindered by past filters that were now destroyed. For the first time in his life, he can see clearly.

Refining Reflection

God knew this process might be hard for us—to drop a filter and walk away unfettered often seems like an impossible task because we have lived with these obstructions for so long. They shaped who we are and how we think. Just as God gave Paul exactly what he needed on the road to Damascus, He provides exactly what we need, as well: His Word.

Throughout this study, we will begin to recognize and challenge filters that do not belong in order to gain footing in our battle and remove them for good. Remember, they were never meant to be there.

Consider the labels listed below and think about what God's Word says. These labels distort our vision, and left unchecked, they can shackle us like prisoners to the enemy's lies, destroying the identity God created for us.

When the Enemy Says I'm:	God Says:
Weak	2 Corinthians 12:9 _____
Unlovable	Isaiah 43:4_____
Defeated	Romans 8:37 _____
Trapped by my past	2 Corinthians 5:17 _____
Unwanted	Isaiah 43:1 _____
Outcast	1 Peter 2:9 _____

Which label have you carried too long? Surrender it to Jesus and claim the truth of His vision, asking Him to allow you to step into the vision He has for you._____

_____

_____

Additional Notes

_____

_____

_____

_____

_____

_____

_____

_____

_____

_____

_____

_____

_____

Week 2

Day 1

A PRISON CELL PRAYER

The beginning of your transformation story always seems to be the hardest. It is the time when you have to be more intentional than ever in choosing to overcome the flesh, the old identity, and lies. I cannot count the times that I have announced to my husband, "I'm done with chocolate!" (Just kidding—I would never say that.) I have declared, however, that I am done with unhealthy eating and determined to eat only rabbit food until I lose all the baby weight.

After such proclamations, my husband simply smiled. He knew it would likely be a short time until, for one reason or another, I tired of rabbit food and stormed the pantry for something more satisfying. Time and experience have taught him that I am an emotional eater; no matter how unhappy I was with my post-baby body, my willpower is sorely lacking when it comes to comfort food.

When I finally made the shift to healthy eating, he was surprised. Day after day passed, and I stuck to my new routine. Weeks of my consistently following the plan slowly convinced him that I just might be genuinely committed. The real test came on vacation, and I maintained my mindfulness of healthy eating. I had experienced a shift in my vision, but only time and continued transformation would prove that to anyone else.

Paul's transformation was no different. In due course, growth was observed in his leadership, ministry, and reputation—so much that his name started to be recognized with warmth by believers and the contempt of many others. The vision God gave Paul inspired, motivated, and pushed him to his limits; yet he believed every moment was worth it—even during imprisonment and life-or-death situations.

To put this profound change of vision in its proper perspective, we must realize that Paul writes this prayer for the people from a Roman prison cell. The man went from devastating the Church to embracing a devotion to spread the Good News of the Gospel so ardent that, even when his personal outlook was bleak, he was fixed on the message God placed in his heart. As a result, he prays for the same heart enlightenment for his fellow believers in Ephesus.

Consider the Context

So far, we have examined only Paul's initial request for spiritual wisdom and insight; these interworking pieces are just the start of the work Paul asked God to do in the Ephesian believers' hearts.

Today, our scope expands to examine each element of Paul's prayer and how it promotes deeper intimacy with the Father and a vision that is saturated with light and hope.

> For this reason I too, having heard of the faith in the Lord Jesus which exists among you and your love for all the saints, do not cease giving thanks for you, while making mention of you in my prayers; that the God of our Lord Jesus Christ, the Father of glory, may give to you a spirit of wisdom and revelation in the knowledge of Him. I pray that the eyes of your heart may be enlightened, so that you will know what is the hope of His calling, what are the riches of the glory of His inheritance in the saints, and what is the surpassing greatness of His power toward us who believe. These are in accordance with the working of the strength of His might which He brought about in Christ, when He raised Him from the dead and seated Him at His right hand in the heavenly places (Eph. 1:15-20).

The New Living Translation interprets the phrase "that the eyes of your hearts may be enlightened" in verse eighteen as hearts that are "flooded with light"—a vital piece of the puzzle in understanding what it is to have our vision changed and filtered by God.

READ THE FOLLOWING VERSES.

What do we learn from them about the heart?

Romans 10:10 _____

_____

_____

Ephesians 4:18 _____

_____

_____

Scripture teaches that the heart is the place responsible for belief. Romans 10:10 reveals that it is with the heart that a person believes, and Ephesians 4:18 deems the heart to be at fault for unbelief, "being darkened in their understanding, excluded from the life of God because of the ignorance that is in them, because of their hardness of heart."

In this later portion of his letter, Paul compares the new man with the old, recognizing that believers should no longer function as the old man did, which is "in the futility of their mind" (Eph. 4:17). The eye of the heart is the inward vision that both receives and contemplates the light.[1] As the light is received and contemplated, spiritual wisdom begins to be worked (remember, it's active) and grown in the very place that God desires to occupy within us. When the heart is shut off or grows dull, we become unreceptive, causing our

---

1   Robert Jamieson, "Ephesians," *Commentary Critical and Explanatory on the Whole Bible* (Grand Rapids: Zondervan Publishing House, 1997).

ears and eyes to close. If we will only see with our eyes, hear with our ears, and *understand with our hearts*, we will turn and find healing from the God Who sees us (Matt. 13:15).

Dig a little Deeper

The heart is the core of life; it determines what the eyes see, the ears hear, and the mind thinks. If the heart is responsible for our belief, we must allow spiritual light to break up the darkness of our own understanding and bring us life.

READ GENESIS 1:1-3.

What was the first evidence of the Spirit of God's moving in new creation? __

_____

_____

_____

The first evidence of God's Spirit moving was light! We need the light of the knowledge of Jesus to shine in our hearts, in order to develop the infinite spiritual wisdom and revelation that we ask of Him. "For God, who said, 'Light shall shine out of darkness,' is the One who has shone in our hearts to give the Light of the knowledge of the glory of God in the face of Christ" (2 Cor. 4:6). The same God Who spoke into the darkness and created physical light is the same God Who offers spiritual light—the knowledge of the glory of God—not only to open the eyes of our heart but also to allow the light to be received, contemplated, and grown.

READ JOHN 1:1-4.

What does light bring? _____

_____

Life and light go hand in hand. If we want to experience the life God longs to give us, we must allow His light to rush in, unfiltered, and change us from within. Commit today to allowing God's light to break through the darkness that binds you to your own understanding, for it is this darkness that houses the filters that block your God-intended vision.

Refining Reflection

Have you experienced a time when your heart was shut off? What was it like?

_____

How does your own understanding determine your heart's response? _____

_____

How might your response change with God-intended vision? _____

_____

Additional Notes

_____

_____

_____

_____

_____

_____

Day 2

EXPOSURE TO LIGHT

One day, I went with my oldest daughter to a Science, Technology, Engineering, and Mathematics (STEM) Day event at a local museum. She had a project that required attending the event, in addition to writing an essay about something interesting she learned.

We camped out at one particular table to learn as much as we could for the essay. It featured a demonstration and explanation about how light affects ultraviolet beads. The woman giving the presentation held five ultraviolet beads in her hand, all a cloudy white color. When she shined a flashlight on them, the individual beads turned either purple, green, red, blue, or yellow. As she took the flashlight away, the beads returned to cloudy white. The presenter explained that the beads' molecules were bonded together in the cloudy white bead; but exposure to direct light broke that bond, allowing the molecules to spread out and receive more light—causing their true colors to be reflected.

This demonstration exactly illustrates how spiritual light affects our hearts. Without the light of Jesus Christ, the molecules of our hearts—the make-up of who God created us to be—are cloudy. They do not reflect true color; therefore, we do not live up to our true potential in Jesus Christ. When the light is received, those cloudy bonds break; we awaken to see the vision that God Himself has of and for us. We see ourselves the way God does, and our vision changes because the light changes what is reflected. Not only do we begin to see ourselves this way, but we also begin to see everything through the reflection of this new light.

I want to draw your attention to something here that you might have missed: the cloudy white beads at the museum were already surrounded by light. They were out on a table in a well-lit room. Yet just being *surrounded* by light was not enough. They had to receive the light up close for the true colors to reflect.

We cannot simply surround ourselves with light. Going to church, having Christian friends, or reading self-help books are all good things, but they are not enough. If you desire to see the reflection of God's vision, you must constantly and consistently expose your heart to the light of Jesus through personal time with God, communication between your heart and His, and hiding His Word in your heart. This practice begins with accepting His free, no-strings-attached gift of salvation and is worked, refined, and reflected more brilliantly as we continue to expose ourselves to the light of Jesus. Remember, where light is, so is life (John 1:4).

Consider the Context

Death is overcome by the life that Jesus brings; and the darkness of this world—the darkness of our hearts—can be overcome by the light of His presence.

READ JOHN 8:12.

What does Jesus mean when He says those who follow Him will have the light of life? How does this differ from walking in darkness? _____

_____

_____

_____

_____

Since the beginning, when God created the heavens and earth, a duality of light and darkness, good and evil, existed. This duality does not contain an equal balance; rather, it reveals God's explicit Sovereignty over the opposition. To make clear His absolute authority and supremacy over darkness, God's Word alone at Creation was the power that bound darkness (Gen. 1:2-3).[2]

When God spoke the light into being at Creation, He gave a boundary to the darkness, pushing it back and declaring it could go no further. God's power over the darkness is unwavering, and He wants to flood your heart with this same light of creation and push the darkness back. Only then can the eyes of our hearts, the inward vision of the place responsible for belief, be enlightened to see with the vision of faith.

Read the following verses that present the presence of God as light. Then match them to the appropriate description. "The tone of confidence that pervades these passages demonstrates that there is no doubt that God's presence as light will conquer and even eliminate the darkness."[3]

Psalm 18:28	Victory over darkness
Psalm 43:3	Illumines darkness
Isaiah 10:17	Changes darkness
Isaiah 42:16	Devours darkness
Micah 7:8	Provides guidance

Dig a little Deeper

When light is present, darkness flees. It is easy, however, for us to linger in the darkness. Our sin nature draws us to the darkness because we can hide in it. John 3:19 illuminates the fact that "the Light has come into the world, and men loved the darkness rather than the Light, for their deeds were evil." Darkness and evil directly oppose the light and presence of God. But God is

---

2   Judith A. Odor, "Light and Darkness," in *The Lexham Bible Dictionary*, ed. John D. Barry et al. (Bellingham: Lexham Press, 2016).

3   Ibid.

unquestionably Sovereign over the opposition, and we are no longer slaves to it.

READ GALATIANS 4:7.

If we are no longer slaves, what are we? _____

_____

_____

"The eye is the lamp of the body; so then if your eye is clear, your whole body will be full of light. But if your eye is bad, your whole body will be full of darkness. If then the light that is in you is darkness, how great is the darkness" (Matt. 6:22-23). As children of God, we can experience clear vision, but we must surrender that which keeps our eyes darkened and causes our hearts to grow dull.

Consider how your unintended filters affect how you receive and contemplate the Light. _____

_____

_____

_____

Last week, we discussed filters that distort our vision of ourselves. This week, we expand our awareness of filters to ponder how exposure to the Light might change our perspective. Think about past experiences that filter how you see things (yourself, others, or circumstances). Have you been wounded by someone close to you and now see relationships through the filter of distrust or bitterness? Maybe you experienced another form of heartache or hardship that created a filter of depression or anxiety. Dig deep to consider filters and the experiences that created them, recognizing how the filters that distort your vision of yourself also distort your vision of what is around you.

Refining Reflection

Recognizing your filters does not change the experience that created them. It does, however, help you understand how they have affected you and shaped your vision of yourself, God, and others.

What experiences have distorted your vision? _____

_____

_____

How do these experiences affect how you see:

Yourself _____

_____

God _____

_____

Others _____

_____

Ask the Lord to prepare your heart to be flooded with light to expose the bonds of darkness and unleash the true reflection of you as a creation of God.

Additional Notes

_____

_____

Day 3

FLOOD AND FLUSH

Sweet and spicy—that's the loving description I often give of my little redhead. This little bundle of sweet-and-spicy fire is all heart and compassion when it comes to loving others, especially her mama. Her sweetness is so genuine and true that when she shows you her heart, it speaks to your own more profoundly than any words she could utter.

Perception is also a part of her gift. Beyond her healing sweetness, she recognizes when others just need to be loved. As a toddler, it manifested as giving extra snuggles to the nursery worker who was having a rough morning or quietly grabbing your hand and smiling at you. As she gets older, her understanding continues to grow—she shows that sweetness to others without holding back. It is amazing how effective and moving her sweetness is.

And then she has spice. That girl possesses all the spirit, confidence, and stubbornness of a bull. I am constantly in awe of this little fireball's raw ability to stand her ground with ferocity—but it is not merely her confidence that impresses. It is the fact that she lets no one persuade her otherwise, and she defends her territory with every last breath. She minces no words and speaks the absolute, unapologetic truth of the situation. She knows who she is and who she belongs to, and nothing can convince her otherwise.

Oh, that we would all adopt such a sweet-and-spicy persona: the sweetness of love and light with the spice of confident truth. The spiritual warfare we face uses the cloudy darkness of unnatural filters to try to deceive our perception and indoctrinate our fears with falsehood. Our ability to bask in the sweet Light of Jesus becomes more of a struggle, and our confidence in His truth waivers. But when we flood the filters with the sweet Light of Jesus, flushing the lies it exposes, we gain a little spice in our step. Our confidence grows from the true reflection of the creation we are. When we lack spiritual light in the darkness of our heart, we become like Saul, who relied on his own understanding as a Pharisee to drive his vision. Our own understanding is dark and limited, in desperate need of being flooded with the sweetness of the Light of God's presence.

What drives your vision? What filters how you see yourself, others, hard times, good times? Is it the light of Jesus? Or have you, like so many others, fallen prey to the filtered vision of disappointment, discouragement, fear, depression, or anxiety?

These filters are cloudy. They distort the true reflection; nonetheless, we see the cloudy, distorted vision of ourselves that shouts, "I'm not good enough, thin enough, strong enough, or pretty enough. I'm ugly, worthless, and disgusting." As I write these words, my heart breaks because I have been there. I am not trying to encourage you to fight for something I have not had to fight for myself. I know the pain of believing the distorted vision and soul-deep feeling of worthlessness. It trapped me for many years in the darkness of my own heart.

For some of you, this feeling existed before you found Christ. When Christ came into your life, that distortion was rebuked and left behind. Praise the Lord for that! I felt these things even with the knowledge and personal relationship with Jesus Christ. For a period of my life, I allowed other people to viciously distort my vision of myself.

I knew in my head all the right answers of how God saw me, but I could not hold on to that in my heart. Without realizing it, I stopped consistently, constantly exposing myself to the Light. The bonds of darkness held me captive, and I had no idea. Yes, I was a Christian, a sinner saved by grace; but the eyes of my heart had grown dull.

I lost confidence in who God said I was. The fear of not being good enough plagued my every decision, outlook, and desire. As I experienced rejection by people close to my heart, the wound deepened, and the darkness closed in further. I felt others comparing me at every angle. Soon, my own driving force was a comparison game of trying to look as good, as pretty, as fit as the "friends" I had at the time. The comparison was a cancer that ate me up inside. It set a goal I could never achieve because as soon as one thing seemed to measure up, something else took its place.

I am ashamed to say that this cycle continued for years. I lost sight of who I was and what God wanted for me—not what He wanted for everyone else, but for me. I lost sight of the hope of His calling. I desperately needed a flooding of light to help me flush the filters that had become ingrained in my identity.

Consider the Context

We were created with a unique identity, given to us directly from our Creator. That identity encompasses who we were created to be and what we were created to do. It relays our worth and shines light on our purpose. No wonder the enemy targets it so maliciously! If he can attack the core of our existence, then he needs only to sit back and watch us destroy ourselves from within.

READ THE FOLLOWING VERSES.

Consider the truth of our God-given identity in comparison to the distortion our filters create.

Ephesians 2:10 _____

_____

Psalm 139:14 _____

_____

Ephesians 1:3-10 _____

_____

The word translated "workmanship" in Ephesians 2:10 is from the Greek word *poiema*, which is the root for our English word *poem*. Put into context, the message is that God's people are His masterpiece.[4] You are "fearfully and wonderfully made" (Psalm 139:14); chosen; made blameless by Him; redeemed; blessed; forgiven; and a recipient of the riches and grace He lavishes.

Understand that we are not perfect. Sin's stain prevents us from achieving the perfection God created in the garden. We are, however, redeemed and made whole through saving knowledge of Jesus Christ; do not miss the beauty of that. Even before creation, God knew mankind would fall; the created world would need to be restored unto the Creator. He planned to unite all things in the fullness of time (Eph. 1:10). You are His masterpiece, not because of anything you have done but simply because He made you and went to magnificent lengths to restore you to Himself.

God's enlightening of our hearts is not achieved solely by bringing us to a saving knowledge of Jesus Christ. It is an ongoing reception and contemplation of His infinite wisdom and revelation, grown and refined through a full knowledge of Him. It brings with it life-changing vision that removes the scales from the eyes of our hearts, just as the scales were removed from Paul's eyes after his encounter on the Damascus Road. It is letting go of every other filter that could distort our vision and clutching tightly to the vision that was intended to be there by the Creator Himself.

---

4   Dr. David Jeremiah, *The Jeremiah Study Bible: English Standard Version* (New York: Hachette Book Group, Inc., 2019), 1593.

What would your life look like if you lived with this enlightened, focused vision? Mine has been drastically different, and I can promise you that yours will be, also. Hope, inheritance, and the surpassing greatness of the power of God are on the line when it comes to enlightening the eyes of our hearts. When the eyes of our hearts are enlightened by the flooding of spiritual wisdom, we can know the hope of His calling and then begin to understand the riches of the glory of His inheritance in the saints. Finally, we can experience the surpassing greatness of His power toward us who believe (Eph 1:18-19). Consider this flooding of spiritual wisdom.

Dig a little Deeper

READ PROVERBS 9.

Note the juxtaposition between two voices that actively call for our attention; list the differences.

Wisdom_____

_____

Folly _____

_____

The voice of wisdom speaks with strength and security, calling to us from her strong house and inviting us into her prepared banquet. Elegant and gentle, she invites us to come in, promising to bring life by multiplying one's days.

The voice of folly crashes in, brash and ignorant, to extend her own invitation. However, folly brings only deception, feeding the lie that "stolen water is sweet; And bread eaten in secret is pleasant" (vs. 17). Folly's presence brings death.

When two opposing voices vie for our attention with offers that sound the same, how do we know the difference?

READ PROVERBS 9:10.

What is the foundation of wisdom? _____

_____

Wisdom calls from a strong house because her foundation is build on the fear of the Lord: that holy reverence for an all-powerful, all-present, all-knowing God. Knowledge of this Holy One unveils the lies of folly and reveals the life of wisdom. We must spend time with Him, in order for this spiritual wisdom to flood our hearts. We must know Who He is and how He thinks and works.

His words are a beautiful window into His heart for us, His creation. Folly forces filter after filter until our identity is lost and the joy of the Lord seems like an unattainable dream. Allowing wisdom to flood our hearts with light is the first step in acknowledging and rejecting those filters.

Refining Reflection

As we broaden our awareness of filters, take a moment to consider what filters your vision. Write the first word that comes to mind when you hear the word *perfect.* _____

_____

_____

Fill in the blank with your answer. I'll give you an example:

perfect: <u>body</u>

If I had the <u>perfect body</u>, I would be enough.

Your turn. If I had_____, I would be enough.

Did we hit a chord? How you answered reveals how your vision is filtered. Does it need to change? Do not do yourself a disservice here by trying to fill in the perfect Sunday school answer. We are human and, by nature, are sinful. Admitting that our thinking might need help opens us to the beautiful possibility of healing and transformation. So be honest with yourself—it is time for a reality check.

Whatever we used to fill that blank is exactly what we idolize; in that, we have played the harlot, just as the prophet Hosea depicted Israel. If we are going to ask God for life-changing vision and step into the fullness of an enlightened heart, we must identify and acknowledge what darkens our understanding, using wisdom to shed necessary light. It is time to call out the idol, recognize the lie we used in place of God's truth, and refuse the filter that distorts our vision into something unintended and unwanted by the God Who created us. God wants to remove the filter. His creation needs no filter. Are you ready, daughter of God, for no filter? Let's flood and flush!

Consider your filter from perspective of folly. What lie is it feeding you? ____

_____

_____

_____

_____

If you were to flood that filter with wisdom's light, what truth would you discover? _____

_____

_____

_____

Additional Notes

_____

_____

_____

_____

_____

_____

_____

_____

_____

_____

_____

_____

_____

_____

_____

_____

_____

Week 3

# #

Day 1

THE FILTER OF IDOLS

Time and again, Israel wandered from God and found herself a slave to a master she was never intended to have—and time and again, God redeemed her. This week, we spend time in the book of Hosea. We will begin to see more clearly the idols we have built, how they distort our vision, and how God desires to bring them to utter destruction as He redeems us and restores us to Himself.

Hosea is known for its theme of redeeming love. It is a beautiful story, really, when you consider the big picture of God's unrelenting love for His people. But when you read through it, chapter by chapter, it can become quite dark, as we recognize just how far Israel wandered from the Lord. Israel had let her heart grow dull.

Recently, my kids and I were sitting at the kitchen table, working on our homeschool lessons for the day. They have many breakfast items to choose from at home, all of which they can fix for themselves. This morning, I decided to make myself an omelet. My little redhead begged me to make one for her, so I did. None of the other kids got one—only her.

We sat at the table, enjoying our omelets as we began our schoolwork. She reveled in the fact that she was the only one getting an omelet—something none of her siblings were getting—and she loved it. In the meantime, my older daughter decided to make herself a fruit smoothie. She filled the blender with yogurt, milk, juice, and berries; it was turning into quite the concoction.

As she poured, she realized she had made too much and asked who would like the extra. All three of her siblings pounced on the opportunity, but there was not enough for all three.

I made the executive decision to split it between the two kids who did not have the omelet. My redhead did not find this option to be equitable. I proceeded to remind her that she was the only one that morning who had received an omelet. It seemed only fair that her brother and younger sister get the remainder of the smoothie, at which point she shoved her unfinished omelet away in a huff.

My gift to her was no longer good enough because she was being left out of something else. Her bright mood suddenly soured, and she—focused on the one thing she could not have—became unappreciative of what she had been given. Her own understanding of the situation caused her to see only what she was not getting, rather than the beauty of what she had been given. In the process, she missed out on both.

The idols that come from our own darkened understanding filter our vision in a way that draws our attention to what we do not have, rather than what we have been given by the Creator. We look at other women and see that we do not have their great hair, metabolism, or talent; and we begin to fixate on all those things and how we can get them, rather than noting the beauty and gifts that God intentionally gave us.

The people of Israel fell into this trap repeatedly. They fixated on what others had and decided it was better than what God had given them. They completely lost sight of the fact that they were God's chosen people, diminishing all He had done to redeem and restore them over time. Their preoccupation led them to abandon their covenant relationship with the living God, in search of comfort that would never come from the carvings of manmade idols. As they sought fulfillment within their own darkened understanding, their hearts grew even darker. The filters that slid in place took them further from the truth.

We see this portrayed through the life of Gomer, a prostitute to whom God sent the prophet Hosea to marry. She was used as a representation of Israel. The New Living Translation (NLT) expresses God's command to Hosea as, "'Go and marry a prostitute, so that some of her children will be conceived in prostitution. This will illustrate how Israel has acted like a prostitute by turning against the Lord and worshipping other gods'" (Hos. 1:2).

The Israelites' hearts and minds were so engrossed in giving to idols what should have been reserved for God alone that He ordered the steps of the prophet Hosea to show Israel her hateful, devastating sin. The idolatry was hurtful to His heart, not to mention an insult akin to spitting in His face—much the same as if the wife of a devoted husband took a lover. Yet the Lord did not turn His back on His people; instead, He sent Hosea into Gomer's path as a living illustration of His unrelenting love, "unmerited goodness, and unwearied patience"—a stark difference from Israel's "perverseness and ingratitude."[5]

Consider the Context

READ HOSEA 1:1-2.

What do we learn about Hosea? _____

_____

_____

What do we learn about the message that comes through the book of Hosea?

_____

_____

5   Matthew Henry and Thomas Scott, "Hosea 1:1," in **Matthew Henry's Concise Commentary** (Oak Harbor: Logos Research Systems, 1997).

"The word of the Lord which came to Hosea" introduces Hosea as having Divine authority and a Divine message (Hos. 1:1). As we see through the Old Testament prophets, God speaks to His people to fulfill the redemptive story. Not much else is known about Hosea, but his obedience in proclaiming God's words to a fallen Israel and marrying a woman who would be unfaithful demonstrates his love and devotion to the Lord.

Right at the outset, God instructs Hosea to marry a prostitute. What a harsh way to be introduced into the narrative! Yet from the beginning, the label of *prostitute* remains central to the story. Who was the woman? I believe we will draw beautiful depth from God's message here when we consider the real-life people of the story, the struggle they faced, and the eventual outcome.

READ HOSEA 1:3.

What is the prostitute's name? _____

Despite her introduction as a prostitute, Gomer was likely a pure bride who strayed to other men after marrying Hosea and was forsaken as a result of this adultery. Had she been a known prostitute at the time of their marriage, that rejection would have been unreasonable.[6] It is incredible enough to think Hosea might choose to marry Gomer in the midst of her sin; but he intentionally wed her as a pure bride, knowing what heartache her future choices would bring.

God created mankind as a pure bride, knowing what we would become, the idols we would fall to, and what it would cost Him to redeem us. The choice to move forward with creation, despite our eventual failures, reveals His desire for relationship with us and His unrelenting love for His creation. This knowledge should help us develop a deeper understanding of the tremendous

---

6   John MacArthur, *The MacArthur Study Bible* (La Habra: The Lockman Foundation, 2006), 1226.

hurt and sadness the Lord experiences when we chase after things other than Him. The anguish increases when those things distort our understanding and continue to draw us further away from the light of God's presence.

Dig a little Deeper

READ HOSEA 2:1-13.

A dull heart lacks the foresight of consequences; yet consequences of great severity ensue. Consider the consequences of Gomer's chasing after her lovers.

_____

_____

_____

While we can delineate many consequences (loss of relationship, joy, and blessing; shame, misperception), I want to draw your attention back to the later part of verse three, "I will also make her like a wilderness."

The depth of this phrase ties directly into the tension between our created purpose versus our unintended path. Isaiah 22:1 calls Jerusalem "the valley of vision"—a place of rich spiritual substance. Agriculturally, it is a land where roots can run deep, producing rich, full growth. This place offers fertile ground for spiritual insight and a depth of knowledge of God; yet a wilderness is the result of Israel's waywardness.

In Scripture, the wilderness is a place of consequence, where nothing of substance can grow. It is good only for pasturing cattle. The Israelites wandered in the wilderness for forty years as a result of their sin of idol worship. Although she was created to be spiritually fertile, her unintended path changed her identity and allowed nothing of substance to flourish.

The same thing happens when our dull hearts, led astray by manmade idols, try to operate through filtered vision.

According to Hosea 9:1-9, what do we experience in the wilderness? _____

_____

_____

_____

In this wilderness, we experience loss of joy (Hos. 9:1-2), exile from our fertile ground, and slavery to the filters that led us there (9:3-6), and ultimately a loss of spiritual discernment (9:7-9). We were not created to exist here; yet our idols—our sins—filter our vision, so the path we believe is right for us is actually nothing more than a wilderness of loss.

Within this wilderness, we fail to see where we are supposed to exist; that place becomes an out-of-reach idea that we do not even know we should strive for. Our perception of where blessings come from is skewed when we believe, as Gomer did, that provision and comfort come from the idols we have fallen to.

We are not so bold to say that we have fallen so low or live so far from the purpose we were created to fulfill. We try to justify our choices and reason our way into the brighter areas of gray, so we do not feel we are planted firmly in the darkness. But these maneuvers are all a part of the skewed perception as we reject the Lord's instruction. When Israel rejected it, she could no longer serve His intended purpose for her: to serve as His priest to the nations (Hos. 4:6). When we reject or forget the Lord's instruction, we lose a vital piece of ourselves—the part that enables us to fulfill our purpose.

Refining Reflection

What threatens to pave your way right into the wilderness? You were meant to exist in a place of beautifully rich spiritual substance, insight, and growth. Are you there? Or is your wilderness nipping at your heals and draining you of the substance and richness you were meant for?

Think about your idols—the things that call your attention away from your covenant relationship with the living God. Idols of addiction, gossip, vanity, physical pleasures, or "eye candy" are foolish, futile, and senseless. Call them out and tear them down. Destroy the filter by surrendering them to the power of the Almighty God. He created you with purpose, and He can easily demolish the things that would keep you from it.

What would calling out and tearing down your filters look like? Compare your wilderness to the path of rich, spiritual substance God longs to lead you through. _____

_____

_____

_____

_____

_____

_____

_____

_____

_____

_____

_____

Day 2

HOW DID WE GET HERE?

Have you ever experienced a moment of clarity—or maybe absolute confusion—in which you ask, "How in the world did I get here?" You did not wake up one morning, in the richness of spiritual wisdom, and decide to walk away from it all. In fact, many of us probably cannot pinpoint the exact moment one idol or another captured our attention. You do not recognize how you got so deep into the wilderness and, consequently, so far from your created purpose; but at some point along the way, the Lord had to let you go there.

Yes, you read that correctly: the Lord had to *let you go there*. I never fully understood this concept until my son entered seventh grade. This boy of mine loves socializing, sports, and fun; academics pose an inconvenient annoyance. That year, I continued as I had for many years before—basically, acting as his personal secretary, so he did not miss assignments or perform poorly on tests.

Soon, I began to feel as though I were the student, working harder and caring more about passing grades than he did until it dawned on me that I had already passed seventh grade! I was doing a disservice to my son by putting in so much effort, when he had yet to learn the lesson he truly needed: his actions (or inactions) have consequences. If he continued to reject my admonitions to do the work to pass seventh grade, I would have to let him fail. I would have to *let him go there*.

Today, we spend time in Hosea 4, where we see the Lord decide to leave Israel alone because of her choices; He removes His restraining grace and allows her to face the full results of them. "When sinners reject Him and are bent on fulfilling their wicked purposes, God removes restraining grace and turns them over to the results of their perverse choices."[7]

Consider the Context

READ ROMANS 1:18-32.

What is the Lord's case against the inhabitants of the land (vv. 1-2)? _____

_____

_____

What resulted from their actions and lack of knowledge of God (v. 3)? _____

_____

_____

God chose Israel to be His priest to the nations. What did they lose by rationalizing and denying their wrongdoing (vv. 4-11)? _____

_____

_____

The deeper God's people venture into their wilderness, the more prominent the mindset of idolatry becomes. They lose their righteous understanding, without which the people are ruined. They become like a stubborn calf that the Lord chooses to abandon to a wilderness of their own making, rather than continue to corral them. Failing to recognize

---

7   MacArthur, "John."

they have become lost in a vast wilderness, they continue to stumble on in their own strength.

What does Isaiah 40:30 say about relying on our own strength? _____

_____

_____

Depending on youth, vigor, or personal strengths only leads us deeper into the wilderness; and we must remember that this is a choice. We have been given knowledge of a holy God yet choose to believe the lies of corruptible man, exchanging the truth of God for lies.

Our filters are lies that become the idols we consult and believe more than we cling to the words of God. We walk away from God's glory; and unfortunately, like the stubborn calf, God sometimes has to let us go to the wilderness we create.

Dig a little Deeper

READ ROMANS 1:18-32.

How does God feel about our stubbornness and rejection (v. 1)? _____

_____

_____

List seven ways God's people reject Him (vv. 21-27). _____

_____

_____

_____

When filters go unchecked, our understanding becomes so foolish that it distorts everything we should recognize as truth, and the Lord's anger ignites. His wrath in these verses is over the fact that the people knew better, yet they continued to do the opposite. "They exchanged the truth of God for a lie, and worshiped and served the creature rather than the Creator" (Rom. 1:25).

This example relates to our vision of ourselves: we know what God says about us, but we do not honor that truth. We become futile in our own speculations, and our foolish hearts become darkened. This action leads us to replacing the truth of God with a lie. Our worship—our devotion, focus, consideration of what is worthy—shifts to the created rather than the Creator. What we see of ourselves or think we should be becomes an idol. Our service follows suit, consumed by worldly attempts to mold ourselves into that false vision. Other idols move in as our attention turns to worldly things that we mistakenly look to for comfort or joy. Focusing on the created, we devise our own definitions of worth, value, happiness, and contentment—all things we strive to attain but can never quite manage to achieve.

Recognizing this erroneous focus, we must intentionally turn our eyes to the Creator, Who is unlike any other being in Heaven or earth.

Refining Reflection

Spend time meditating on the passages listed below. Remember, "the fear of the Lord is the beginning of wisdom, and the knowledge of the Holy One is insight" (Prov. 9:10)! Let His Word and the reminders of His great depth of character and attributes be a flood of light.

ATTRIBUTES OF GOD:

Isaiah 43:15: _____

_____

I Peter 4:19: _____

_____

Isaiah 9:6: _____

_____

Psalm 145:17: _____

_____

I John 4:8: _____

_____

Malachi 3:6: _____

_____

I Samuel 2:2: _____

_____

I John 3:20: _____

_____

Psalm 90:2: _____

_____

Hebrews 13:8: _____

_____

Job 42:2: _____

_____

Romans 11:33: _____

_____

Psalm 147:5: _____

_____

Ephesians 6:10: _____

_____

Titus 1:2: _____

_____

Psalm 102:12: _____

_____

Psalm 86:15: _____

_____

As we hold these sacred truths in our hearts, the distortions of our filters begin to break apart. We realize that we, the created, are designed to reflect the beauty and brilliance of the Creator Himself. Eventually, we may even begin to see those things that we despise about ourselves as intricately placed details, carved by the Master Himself, for the purpose of bringing glory to Him alone.

May we stop replacing the truth of God with lies, see Him more clearly, and reflect Him more brilliantly! As we transform into this beautiful reflection, darkness flees; filters shatter; and idols fall.

How did we come to be in a wilderness? Somewhere along the way, our sinful nature replaced "the truth of God with a lie" (Rom. 1:25). It is time to leave the wilderness behind and step into the Promised Land, where spiritual insight runs deep and our knowledge of God matures us toward new heights of understanding and new reflecting potential.

Consider the attributes of God. What lies about God and His character might be keeping you from leaving the wilderness? Expose them and mindfully work to replace them with the truth and glory of God. _____

_____

_____

_____

Need a little help with today's verses? Some of my own interpretations of the attributes are as follows:

- # Isaiah 43:15: holy, King
- # I Peter 4:19: faithful
- # Isaiah 9:6: Wonderful Counselor, Mighty God, Eternal Father, Prince of Peace
- # Psalm 145:17: righteous, kind
- # I John 4:8: love
- # Malachi 3:6: constant, never-changing
- # I Samuel 2:2: holy, Rock
- # I John 3:20: all-knowing
- # Psalm 90:2: everlasting
- # Hebrews 13:8: unchanging
- # Job 42:2: all-powerful
- # Romans 11:33: all-knowing
- # Psalm 147:5: abundant in power
- # Hebrews 6:10: just
- # Titus 1:2: never lies

\#   Psalm 102:12: enthroned forever

\#   Psalm 86:15: merciful, gracious, slow to anger, abounding in steadfast
    love and faithfulness

Additional Notes

_____

_____

_____

_____

_____

_____

_____

_____

_____

_____

_____

_____

_____

_____

_____

_____

_____

_____

Day 3

A RESTORING JOURNEY HOME

What if I were to tell you that great beauty can exist in the wilderness? "Therefore, behold, I will allure her, Bring her into the wilderness And speak kindly to her" (Hos. 2:14). To speak kindly, or tenderly, is a phrase that denotes a wooing, speaking to her heart. Sometimes, God has to bring us into a wilderness, away from all that we know, are comfortable with, and are distracted by so He can woo us. He does so by speaking directly to the source responsible for our belief.

Israel was guilty and deserved great punishment for her abandonment of God. She could not escape the consequences of her actions, just as we cannot. But God's love for His people is so great that He steps in and saves us from destruction, speaking to our hearts so personally that we cannot help but be moved into intimate relationship with Him once again.

Today, we explore this beautiful process of wooing. After God brings us into the wilderness and speaks tenderly to our hearts, His blessings begin to return; and hope is offered. Oh, sweet hope! It truly changes everything. Our idolized filters suffocate us, reducing our outlook to one of destruction and despair; but God wants to woo us out of that darkness and give us hope for a future in which darkness will not overtake the light. He wants us to accept that we are someone of worth, meant for greater purpose than the limits our filters bind us to.

As God woos Israel in her wilderness, hope begins to illuminate the path back to His intended purpose for her, His blessings over her, and His goodness to her. This hope sparks Israel's restoring journey home; ours will be no different.

Consider the Context

READ HOSEA 2:14-23.

What position is being restored to Israel? _____

_____

_____

What blessings are being restored to Israel? _____

_____

_____

How is the goodness of God being restored to Israel? _____

_____

_____

The Valley of Achor in verse fifteen refers to a valley just outside of Jericho, known as the valley of trouble. It was here that Achan was punished after disobeying God's order and took spoils from the destruction of Jericho. This judgment made things right once again for Israel and led her to fruitful victories against her enemies, painting the Valley of Achor as a doorway to hope.

In His grace and mercy, the Lord allows us to face punishment of sin and find hope that we can move from it into right relationship with Him, as portrayed in verse sixteen: "'It will come about in that day,' declares the LORD, 'That you will call Me Ishi And will no longer call Me Baali.'"

The term *Ishi* is equivalent to "husband," whereas *Baali* reflects the position of a master. Returning to a right relationship with the Lord means we move from the relationship of master and slave and return to affection and intimacy between our heart and His. Israel lost that because she forgot her true Love, her true God. To restore it, God declares that she would forget her lovers, her false gods, by the wooing of her first love. He took it beyond the outward obedience of the Law and activated the inner response of the heart. However, God knew that our sinful condition renders our hearts to be "more deceitful than all else" (Jer. 17:9). What could not be achieved by simple outward conformity to the Old Covenant, God provides through the New Covenant by means of a new, regenerated heart.[8]

As the Mediator of the New Covenant between God and man, Jesus regenerates and renews our hearts in order to woo us unto Himself and restore the relationship we were meant to have with the Creator. Can our idols do that? Can they speak to the heart so intimately or restore us so fully? No, but the Creator does. Although He is the One we have broken and hurt with our unfaithfulness, He brings us back, connects with our hearts, and produces a change so deep that the labels sin attached to us are destroyed; and we are given a new name.

This restoration of relationship brought Israel to a place of honor once again. She was no longer known as a prostitute, and it was not because of anything she had to offer. Israel brought nothing to the union; God offered all the promises and paid the dowry. A new identity is given in our restoration. Although we bring nothing to the marriage, He does not hold it over us. Instead, the betrothal is founded in righteousness, justice, lovingkindness, compassion, and faithfulness. In paying the dowry we do not deserve, He changes our identity and gives us value that we have never given ourselves. He brings us out of slavery and into intimacy by wooing our sinful, broken

---

8   Ibid, 1229.

hearts. He provides healing and generates a new heart through the redemption that only Jesus offers.

Dig a little Deeper

READ HOSEA 3.

"'Go again, love a woman who is loved by her husband, yet an adulteress, even as the Lord loves the sons of Israel, though they turn to other gods and love raisin cakes'" (vs. 1). This unrelenting, redeeming love for His people is so deeply rooted in the heart of the Father that He did not want the words merely spoken by the prophet—He wanted a tangible example. So he called Hosea, the man, to go again to Gomer, the woman, and redeem her.

How is God's command to Hosea different here than the command in chapter one? _____

_____

_____

What did God say Israel would dwell without for many days (vv. 3-4)? _____

_____

_____

Israel's nationhood, priestly garments, and objects of worship mattered greatly to her identity; but God did not want her identity to be wrapped up in things she put so much stock in. He wanted her to find herself directly in Him. Having to dwell without these things was a beautiful opportunity for Israel to let go of the identity that was tied to traditional comforts and embrace the Creator Himself. As a result, she would discover exactly who God created her to be and the purpose she was created to fulfill.

I find it interesting that the Lord's first command to Hosea was to go *take* a wife, but His second command is to go *love*. This example is not merely one of the Lord's ability and willingness to get us out of our own trouble. It is a yearning for us and a promise that His love for us is not determined by our worth; rather, our worth is determined by His love for us.

Idols and filters would have us believe otherwise. They lead into wilderness, trapping us in a place that lacks substance and depth. The Lord, in His love, will allow us to go there; but His goodness will not leave us there. He will have nothing to do with idols; we must, therefore, leave them in the wilderness and allow our hearts to respond to the Creator, as He floods us with the light of His presence and power. Idols hold no power; filters hold no truth. Past sins and present choices do not define us. The wooing love of the One Who created us does.

Will we recognize the wilderness as a place of wooing? Or will we become distracted or bitter with the wilderness? May we have eyes to see and ears to hear the wooing of the Savior!

Refining Reflection

Consider how traditional comforts affect your identity. What would it look like to leave them behind and truly seek the face of God? _____

_____

_____

_____

_____

_____

_____

Additional Notes

_____

_____

_____

_____

_____

_____

_____

_____

_____

_____

_____

_____

_____

_____

_____

_____

_____

Week 4

Day 1

WHAT IS THE HOPE
OF HIS CALLING?

"I pray that the eyes of your heart may be enlightened, so that you will know what is the hope of His calling" (Eph. 1:18). As our hearts are enlightened, idols forsaken, and filters shattered, we can know and experience "the hope of His calling." But what is this hope? Paul knew his prayer for this heart-enlightened vision was a gateway to reveal to us the hope of God's calling on our lives. I am sure we are all familiar with that word, *calling*. It has been a source of simultaneous inspiration and frustration my entire life! I have wondered what my calling is many times. What purpose did God give me? What is He calling me to do in this life?

Sometimes, these questions excite me, as things line up and lead me closer to realizing hopes of what I want to do. In other chapters of life, it has haunted me when I find myself on my knees once again in utter desperation for direction. It is usually in this place that the Lord gently rebukes me and reminds me that I have it all wrong—while I focused on the *doing*, I forgot about *being*. The "hope of His calling" includes both what I am to do *and* be. While the calling of a profession or vocation is a huge part of the bigger picture, we cannot do *what* we were called to do until we are *who* we were called to be.

Expanding this concept of calling can be overwhelming when we try to consider every facet it involves. First, we must understand that "the hope of

His calling" simply begins with recognizing the hope that comes from being called, or invited, into the kingdom of God. We were called out of a life of sin and shame into His marvelous light! Scripture clearly asserts that we all need rescue because "all have sinned and fall short of the glory of God" (Rom. 3:23).

We are called out of literal darkness. I was first called out of this darkness as a five-year-old girl. After attending church since birth, I knew I was a sinner who needed Jesus. I believed that God loves me so much He sent His only begotten Son, Jesus, to die on a cross for me to pay the debt of my sin. The beauty of His resurrection, His absolute defeat of death, is the beauty he offers me in His gracious gift of salvation.

Consider the Context

Do not take the beauty of God's gracious gift for granted. We must consider our condition before, upon, and after salvation in order to genuinely grasp the fullness of being called into God's kingdom.

READ ROMANS 3:10-18.

Paul declares that Jews and Gentiles alike are guilty before God. Identify the fourteen indictments listed against man.

v. 10: _____

_____

v. 11: _____

_____

v. 12 (includes three): _____

_____

_____

_____

v. 13 (includes three): _____

_____

_____

_____

v. 14: _____

_____

v. 15: _____

_____

v. 16: _____

_____

v. 17: _____

_____

v. 18: _____

_____

READ ROMANS 3:21-31.

After proving the impossibility of man's achieving righteousness, Paul shifts his argument to the provision of righteousness from God Himself.

Does God make distinctions among sinners (vv. 22-23)? _____

_____

_____

We have all missed the mark. God makes no distinction between your sin and mine nor between your background and mine. Your sin does not make you fall any lower than anyone else does. Our filters make distinctions, leading us to constantly try to atone for ourselves. They manipulate and deceive us into thinking either that our sin is not as bad as the girl's next door or into believing that real forgiveness is unattainable. Both directions lead straight to a wilderness that keeps us from experiencing the fullness of the hope of His calling.

READ ROMANS 6:23.

What does God's redemption cost us? _____

_____

_____

_____

_____

_____

Understanding our position in sin and our raw inability to remedy it, God knew that saving His creation was up to Him. He loves us so much that He paid the debt with the blood of Jesus—a sacrifice needed only once but covered every sin. This is the authority from which He calls us into His kingdom—a calling that, upon acceptance, draws the believer into a covenant relationship with Him where condemnation no longer exists (Rom. 8:1). We need only confess our sins and believe in our hearts that He is Lord (Rom. 10:9). In Christ, we are free; stop carrying the guilt of the past.

Understanding this truth was my first glimpse of the hope that comes with being called into the kingdom of God. I am rescued from a debt I can never repay, and I now have hope as a child of God. While I believe that nothing I could ever do can change my security in Christ, and I will never again experience the darkness from before being saved by grace, I recognized that darkness remains something I battle. It is a different kind of darkness, though—it is the darkness of being trapped in my own head, which casts a horrible shadow over my heart and vision. In this darkness, I lost sight of "the hope of His calling."

Dig a little Deeper

After accepting the call into the kingdom of God, we receive the gift of the Holy Spirit, Who dwells in us and guides our will, thoughts, and choices. We are given the ability to see things in a new light and to walk confidently in the truth of God, rather than blindly stumble our way through the darkness of living without the Spirit.

However, we must choose to fix our minds on the things of the Spirit, even though we have access to the light as new creatures in Christ. We must choose to use and develop this new vision. When we fail to exercise it, we slip back into old thoughts that are steeped in darkness.

READ ROMANS 8:5-6.
What is the result of a mind that is set on the flesh? _____

_____

_____

What is the result of a mind that is set on the Spirit? _____

_____

_____

As a teenager, I was happy and confident. I knew who I was and never doubted the qualities I had nor talents God gave me. I would describe my upbringing as having a mind set on the Spirit. But as many of you have experienced, life happened. I went to college, followed by graduate school. My husband and I married, started having babies, tried to begin our career paths, and worked to achieve the white picket fence ideal. But a subtle darkness slowly began to circle my heart.

After my first child was born, my body was—well, it was not what it used to be. This new reality shook my confidence to the core. Deep-rooted body issues and shame took hold. Embarrassed about how I looked, I felt worthless as a woman. Over the next two years, we experienced the devastating losses of two miscarriages—again, worthless.

Unfortunately, I surrounded myself with "friends" who dragged me deeper into the darkness by focusing on the exterior worth I did not possess. They were thinner, fitter, more glamorous, and more confident. I allowed myself to be sucked into their comparison game, in which worth depended entirely on measuring up to their standard of beauty, talent, and popularity.

I failed to realize what was happening. My value was based on a vision I had of myself and what I needed to change. My mind was *aware* of the Spirit, but, in all transparency, it was *set* on the flesh. My hope was fleeting, and my idol became a manmade perception that I needed to achieve. My focus shifted from what God had created me to be. I became depressed and quite adept at putting on a show for the people around me. Everyone thought I was that sweet, confident girl they knew from back in the day; but inside, I hurt. I felt that my value relied on what I did to look better and whether it appeared as though I had it all together. It was exhausting.

After my third child was born, my marriage suffered a devastating blow that crushed me. I firmly believe the darkness would have consumed me, if not for the grace of God. I was lost in a wilderness with no idea how to find my way out. Hope was a concept far too dangerous to cling to. Somewhere in the midst of my wilderness of pain, fear, and absolute brokenness, I felt the Lord pick me up and wipe away the tears. He began to woo me. Just as a parent holds a child's face to direct her where to look, God guided my eyes directly to Him. He knew I needed my vision flooded with light, so I could begin to flush away the filters that were tearing me apart.

My Lord's unrelenting love began to flood the filters. It was a slow process; I could not have taken it all in, had it been any other way. Slowly, the hope I experienced, being called into the kingdom of God, revealed how God sees me. It reflected who I am in God's vision. Let me tell you, it vastly differed from my own.

I would like to tell you that it took only one glimpse of God's vision to change my perspective and overcome the years of hurt and brokenness, but it did not. I say this to dispel any pretense that the process is easy-peasy, lemon-squeezy! On the contrary, it is a daily battle that you must choose to fight—but, oh, consider the vast difference you might see if you allow your gaze to fall directly where the Lord points you! What a difference it could be for you, your family, and your community if you allow your vision to be directly exposed to the light of Jesus, breaking the bonds of darkness and reflecting His beautiful, shining creation!

This is "the hope of His calling"—that we are more than this world understands and more than conquerors in the name of Jesus. We reflect the beauty of the Creator Himself. We have a glorious hope in life—not as the world sees it, but as God intended it. Did God call us to live this life with fear and darkness? No, He calls us by name and reveals what He sees, so we can experience "the hope of His calling."

What is your definition of hope? _____

_____

_____

_____

To hope is to wait or look for something with eager expectation. Incorporating God's redemptive acts with our trusting hearts nurtures confidence and allows us to know the fullness of God's goodness now and in what lies ahead. This biblical hope differs vastly from that of the world.

In Greek philosophy, the concept of hope is something that humans are capable of, yet limited in. Their hope reflected both good and bad experiences; therefore, the future that one could hope for was limited by one's individual possibilities. "Biblical hope avoids this subjectivity by being founded on something that provides a sufficient basis for confidence in its fulfillment: God and His redemptive acts as they culminate in the birth, life, death, and resurrection of Jesus Christ."[9]

My hope was so fleeting in my wilderness because it was based on my own subjective possibilities, rather than being rooted in the confident expectations of God's fulfilling His promises. The hope that Paul prays for in Ephesians is one of trust and confidence. The Greek word used is a noun that conveys the expectation of what is sure to come and the active, faith-filled waiting for God to fulfill His promises. "Now may the God of hope fill you with all joy and peace in believing, so that you will abound in hope by the power of the Holy Spirit" (Rom. 15:13). Throughout Scripture, God is presented as the Source of hope.

Refining Reflection

Filters limit hope within the boundaries of our own subjective possibilities: those things that we, in our darkened understanding, can see a pathway toward, based on what we have experienced. The hope God offers has no use for subjective thoughts. It objectively focuses on Him as Creator and Redeemer, He Who is all-knowing, all-powerful, and all-present. When we plant ourselves in this hope, we see the calling and rejoice in it. We see

---

9   Ben Craver, "Hope," in *The Lexham Bible Dictionary*, ed. John D. Barry, et al. (Bellingham: Lexham Press, 2016).

who we are called to be—daughters of the King who have been called into the kingdom of God, never to roam alone nor be forever lost in a wilderness. We are loved, called by name, wooed, and restored to the beautiful creation He purposed. "The hope of His calling" gives a clear, unfiltered perspective of who we were in our darkness and who we are as we transform in the realization of who He created us to be. This hope knows no limits—only the trustworthiness of God and a flooded heart that is willing to believe.

Spend a few moments today using your Bible's concordance to look up the word *hope*. Search the verses listed to find Scriptures that show God as the Source of hope. Write one of them below and meditate on it this week. ____

_____

_____

_____

_____

_____

_____

_____

_____

_____

_____

_____

Day 2

HOPE IN THE CALLING

I love the story of Gideon in the book of Judges. We see a beautiful example of the hope of God's calling from darkness and revealing of His vision of Gideon. You might remember the fleece he put out, asking for a sign, or maybe the fact that God used him and only three hundred men to defeat the Midianite army without raising a sword. But do you remember how Gideon's story begins?

Before we meet Gideon, we see in Judges 6:1-10 that Israel was delivered into the hand of the Midianites because she did evil in the sight of the Lord. The Midianites prevailed against and oppressed Israel. By *oppressed*, I mean absolutely crushed down. They were a terrifying foe—not merely a stronger nation set on domination but a merciless one. Every year, they destroyed all the crops and cattle, leaving nothing to sustain the Israelites. Scripture says that the children of Israel made dens, caves, and strongholds in the mountains to hide.

In Numbers 31:1-18, Moses is instructed to take vengeance on a certain clan of Midianites for their part in seducing Israel to sin. War ensues, and Israel spares only virgin women and female children. Other Midianite clans resent Israel for this slaughter and become the source of a dominating oppression against Israel. The book of Judges records that they came in "as numerous as locusts, and their camels were without number" (7:12). They take what they want, destroy the rest, and leave Israel impoverished.

This persecution has lasted seven years when we finally meet Gideon. It is the daily reality and the filter through which the Israelites view everything. Judges 1:6 says that God had given them over to the hands of the Midianites. In our redemptive cycle, we know that when God gives His people over, it is only a matter of time before the wooing begins. But He must allow them to experience the wilderness, filters and all, to appreciate the flood of light that is to come.

Consider the Context

Gideon lives in fear, seeing himself as nothing more than a weak man who hides in shadows. When he first comes on the scene, we get a vastly different picture of him than those heroic tales herald.

What is Gideon doing when we first meet him? (Jgs. 6:11) _____

_____

_____

There is Gideon—hiding in the shadows, beating out wheat in the winepress to save it from the Midianites. This picture automatically gives us the understanding of his distress. The fact that he beats the wheat himself suggests a small amount of grain, since the common practice of the day was to have the cattle tread it. This paltry stash starkly represents all that they had and were desperate to protect. Gideon is not on a threshing floor, up on a platform in the open air to allow the wind to carry away the chaff; he is in a winepress, suggesting he is under a tree out of view. Gideon hides in the shadows of his fearful reality.

When the Angel of the Lord appears and begins to talk with him, his vision is drastically challenged. The Angel of the Lord says, "'The Lord is with you, O valiant warrior'" (Jgs. 6:12). I can just imagine Gideon's double-take, looking around, and thinking, "Who, me?" *Valiant warrior* is not necessarily the vision that Gideon has of himself.

His first response ignores this new title, questioning the idea that the Lord is with them. He clearly knows his history, since he mentions miracles the Lord performed for the Israelites; but he has lived in the wilderness too long to have witnessed them personally. He knows what God is capable of but has lost hope that He will come through for them now. Gideon has no hope of being freed from his oppression. His vision is darkened.

READ JUDGES 6:11-13.

What filters affect Gideon's vision of himself and his situation? _____

_____

_____

Filters like fear, bitterness, hopelessness, weakness, and doubt trap Gideon in the middle of a wilderness of abandonment. What caused his circumstances or how he got there is immaterial to him; he sees only what his filters allow.

Have you ever felt abandoned by the Lord? Explain. _____

_____

_____

Gideon's despondence is devastating. It surpasses the disappointment of not getting something he wanted, like we would be when that new air fryer does not appear under the Christmas tree. He has no confidence his dire situation could change because he does not believe a greater Power will offer help. He thinks he has to rely on his own strength as a man; in the face of the enemy, it is not enough.

As humans do, he adjusts his expectations to what he can reasonably achieve—hide and maybe try to stash away a little wheat from the enemy's plundering, so his family does not starve. He holds no hope for something greater ahead, far less of victory or change. Instead, he makes his wilderness as comfortable as possible because hoping for more is out of the question.

Dig a little Deeper

READ JUDGES 6:14-16.

How does God begin to upset Gideon's filters?

Filter of weakness: _____

_____

Filter of abandonment: _____

_____

Filter of inadequacy: _____

_____

Filter of defeat: _____

_____

The beautiful thing about the wilderness is the moment God begins to woo you out of it. Gideon's hopelessness is challenged as the Lord defies every filter Gideon has accepted. To his filter of weakness, the Lord reminds him of the strength given him. To his filter of insignificant identity, God reminds him Who sends him. In the face of his filter of fear, the Lord declares that He will be with Gideon, and victory will be his.

The verses that follow show a hope beginning to stir. Gideon first recognizes that he is, indeed, having a Divine conversation with the God he assumed had abandoned them. He realizes God is setting him on a path to destroy the enemy and bring the Israelites out of fear; however, he questions his own understanding and asks the Lord for a sign that his perception is, in fact, truth from God Himself.

In His wooing of Gideon, God provides the sign he needs by igniting the meal Gideon offered into flames. Gideon is drawn to humility. God Himself is calling Gideon out of the wilderness. At that, Gideon's hope is restored as he acknowledges and accepts God's presence: a process that took time and evidence directly from God. His newfound hope understands that the nation of Israel is still God's chosen people and will be delivered from the enemy; that Gideon himself is, by God's grace, more than the sum of his filters; and, most of all, that God Himself is present with him and more powerful than the innumerable foe they faced. Gideon was called by God as an Israelite, a child of God; now he is also called to be a vessel through which God will work mightily.

Refining Reflection

You have been called by the Redeemer into the kingdom of God. The first step in experiencing the hope that comes with that is to respond to it. Have you responded to the call that will pull you out of the darkness of sin and secure your place in God's kingdom? Nothing is more glorious than that response. In the moment you accept the invitation, you are guaranteed the presence of God for eternity. Throughout Scripture, God promises never to leave nor forsake His people. When you accept the invitation, you are His. His promises are true for you.

Spend time today reflecting on the hope that comes with this initial calling into the kingdom of God. Do not get distracted with the calling of the *doing* just yet; focus on the hope of *being* a child of God.

As a child of God, what hope do you have?

In circumstances: _____

_____

In relationships: _____

_____

In your future: _____

_____

In the face of your filters: _____

_____

Receive this hope through the eyes of your heart. Allow your inward vision and contemplation of truth to enlighten and flood your heart. Do not skip over this exercise as something that is insignificant. Instead, allow it to be worked and developed into your belief center, so it brings you to your knees in worship. The God of the universe, Creator, and Redeemer chose you. You are invited to dine with the King, to embrace Him in relationship, and to be restored to the treasure He created you to be. Let that hope stir you to what lies ahead.

Additional Notes

_____

_____

_____

_____

_____

Day 3
THE HOPE IN THE DOING

The hope of *being* must be secured within our hearts before the hope of *doing* can flourish. The *being* enables the *doing*; therefore, *who* He has called us to be provides a foundation for *what* He calls us to do. Only when Gideon acknowledges who he is in the light of God's presence is he ready for what is to come. His identity changes significantly. As a man, he is inconsequential; in the presence of God, he is a valiant warrior—a beautiful transformation that was somewhat difficult to understand, accept, and don Notice in Judges 6:14-16 that each time Gideon's filters try to capture his attention and fix his focus on himself, God responds by returning Gideon's vision to Who He is and what He will do.

The hope that comes in embracing who we are called to be encompasses the beauty that God supplies every need, plans every mission, and paves the way to victory. The outcome has nothing to do with me and everything to do with Him. This hope is essential. We cannot move forward in anything God calls us to do until we accept who He has called us to be. Often, when we feel discouraged about what we are called to do, we have lost sight of who we are called to be. The rest of Gideon's story stakes a claim in the truth of who he is in God, and this security enables him to step into what God has called him to do.

For Gideon *the man,* the calling is too much; for Gideon *the child of God,* it is life-changing. The change does not take place overnight. While Gideon's hope is restored and relationship forged, fear still plays a role. He asks for signs at several points when he doubts his own perception of the situation. In each instance, in His continued wooing of Gideon's heart, God grants him the signs he needs and opens Gideon's heart to trust.

Consider the Context

Read the following verses, consider what perception Gideon needs to clarify when he asks for a sign, and discover how God answers.

Judges 6:17-21 _____

_____

_____

_____

Judges 6:36-40 _____

_____

_____

_____

Gideon first asks for clarification in his perception of God. I am sure you have been there. Faced with filters that have deceived us for so long, we can find that our hearts become doubtful when God Himself begins to woo us. Receiving a sign that clearly reveals God, Gideon learns something about himself: the *being* component of his calling. Filters of abandonment are challenged as God reveals Himself.

When God reveals Himself to Gideon, He explains His vision and plan. Gideon begins to move and breathe in his confident hope of Who God is and who he is in light of God, but he finds that he needs clarification in the *doing*; thus, we read of Gideon's fleece experience. It is important to remember that God does not have to give Gideon the signs; He could require that Gideon trust Him. The Creator has nothing to prove to His creation. Yet God gives Gideon the confirmation requested because He continues to woo Gideon out of his wilderness. In the process, He restores both hope and the trust that comes with it.

As God increases Gideon's trust, He readies him for the task ahead. After the first sign reveals Who God is and that He is, indeed, with Gideon, God orders his first mission—to destroy the altar to Baal his father built. Still afraid, Gideon sets out under cover of night, and amazing things result from his obedience. Gideon's family turns to God; his community follows suit, emboldening Gideon to deliver Israel from Midian.

Dig a little Deeper

READ JUDGES 7:1-8.

How many men gathered to fight? _____

How did this number compare with the size of the Midianite forces? _____

_____

Why did God tell Gideon that too many men came to fight? _____

_____

What was the final count of Gideon's fighting men? _____

Can you imagine the gravity of seeing God's people gather for war against an enemy that had oppressed them for so long, knowing they assemble because of you? What an overwhelming thought! And how exciting to see your hope become the hope of so many others!

Gideon is no longer unsure of who he is in God and what God can do—if he were, he could hardly be prepared to weed out the thirty-two thousand men who gathered to fight the innumerable Midianite army. God declares that Gideon has too many men and, by process of elimination, whittles the number to just three hundred because God did not want His children to think they had anything to boast in but God Himself. God communicates a proper vision for His children—their worth, value, talents, and victories all rest in Him. He removes the focus from their perceived strength in numbers and turns it to the strength of the Almighty God.

READ JUDGES 7:9-22.

What filter does God know might try to shadow Gideon's perception of His calling? _____

_____

_____

What does God do to overcome that filter and return Gideon's confident hope?

_____

_____

How does Gideon respond to what he sees in the enemy camp (v. 15)? _____

_____

_____

God gives Gideon one more sign, this time unsolicited. In His goodness, He equips Gideon with confident hope by paving the way to victory even before they march into battle. In this knowledge, Gideon leads his men to drive out the Midianite army without lifting a sword. The enemy knew of

Gideon and the Israelites' God, and they feared—not because Gideon was a dangerous foe but because the God with him is.

Refining Reflection

"The hope of His calling" shifts our focus to the One Who calls us and His promise to carve the path ahead of us. I can accomplish anything He calls me to do because I trust that, as His child, I have access to His power, presence, and promises. Though the path may not always be clear, my confident hope emboldens me to trust that He will reveal what I need to see and enlighten my heart with the wisdom needed to step out in faith.

Spiritual wisdom, revelation in the knowledge of God, a flooded heart—these components work within and mature me to experience the confident hope He calls me to live in.

What might God be calling you to do in which your understanding of *being* affects the *doing*? _____

_____

Are you ready to walk in the confident hope of His calling? Tell Him you are ready and commit your focus to Who He is and what He promises.

Additional Notes

_____

_____

_____

_____

_____

Week 5

Day 1

THE RICHES OF HIS GLORIOUS INHERITANCE

Gideon teaches us that as spiritual wisdom and knowledge of God increases in our flooded hearts, we develop confident hope in Him. We begin to truly understand what we find in Him and He in us: "the riches of the glory of His inheritance in the saints" (Eph. 1:18).

The confident hope Paul refers to in Ephesians 1:18 is the beginning of a much greater, deeper, richer inheritance for believers. This inheritance is reciprocal in its essence, given to the believer and to Jesus Christ. We, the redeemed bride of Christ, are His inheritance; He, the Redeemer, is ours. It is the richness of this inheritance that we focus on this week, so we may better understand the beauty and depth of what comes when we place our confident hope in God.

Throughout Scripture, an inheritance is considered a stable, lasting possession and usually refers to something immovable (i.e., a country, land, house, people). As we move forward in our study of inheritance, think in terms of a will. A will-maker lays out the plan for what will be inherited by whom.

The Old Testament laws of inheritance reserved a double portion for the firstborn son, completely neglecting daughters or illegitimate sons. The only way for an illegitimate son to receive an inheritance was to be adopted as a full son. The Old Testament concept of inheritance continues through the promise of blessing to Abraham and eventually through the covenant established between God and Israel—the Mosaic Covenant.

To best understand the glorious inheritance Paul refers to, we must consider how the Old Covenant between God and Israel differs from the New Covenant brought about by Jesus Christ. Within each covenant was an inheritance, and it is in the New Covenant that we find the riches of His glorious inheritance in the saints.

Consider the Context

From the time of their creation, Adam and Eve experienced what we were always meant to have: direct access to and relationship with God. Can you imagine what it was like to walk through the garden with God Himself, to enjoy His presence and speak with Him face-to-face on a daily basis?

It must have been glorious, yet Adam and Eve knew nothing else. They knew their Creator well, without any barriers. Oh, Eve, how I wish you had thrown that serpent out of your presence the second he began to speak! (It seems like that would be a natural reaction to a talking snake, but I imagine things might have been a bit different in the Garden of Eden. A talking serpent was probably normal.)

When Eve allowed the serpent's words to lure her into sin, the dynamic could no longer be what the Creator originally intended. He could no longer commune so freely with His creation because He cannot be in the presence of sin. What was meant to be theirs was no longer within reach; it became something they could only hope to regain one day. Now more was required to attain what was once freely given by the Creator.

In God's goodness, He killed animals and used the skins to cover the nakedness of Adam and Eve, establishing the requirement of sacrifices to atone for the sins of His creation. Once, they had no need for a covenant, but a new chasm sprang up between Creator and creation that could never be spanned. A covenant was the only way for the Creator to protect, provide for, and commune with His people.

READ EXODUS 19:1-6.

How long has it been since Israel left Egypt? _____

_____

To what does God refer in verse four? What did the Israelites see God do? ___

_____

Identify the "if . . . then" of the covenant in verses five and six. _____

_____

The Mosaic Covenant, established between God and Israel, looked more to the immediate protection and provision God offered His people. Since He originally intended to walk through life with us, it makes perfect sense we need the Creator's protection and provision. As a specific example, God provided the Promised Land for His people; when Israel disobeyed, the inheritance was withheld. They wandered in the wilderness for forty years before even stepping into the Promised Land and beginning their quest to possess it.

Again, consider the will. The will-maker holds the right to choose whom to put in the will and whom to take out of it. He also retains the right to determine the will's terms, allowing the inheritor to remain in good standing with the will-maker, which provides benefit for both will-maker and heir.

The Mosaic Covenant provided a benefit—an inheritance—for both Israel and God. The usual focus when considering this covenant is on the people. If they fulfilled their end, they received the blessings (inheritance) that came with being God's chosen people. In other words, God had a will and—as long as the people obeyed His command—they remained in the will. Have you ever stopped to consider what God defines as His portion in this covenant? It is the people! If the people obey His command, He communes with them and claims them as His own. In the Hebrew text of the Old Testament, Israel is often called "Yahweh's heritage." God stands to gain what He always intended for His creation: relationship.

Through obedience to the Law, the Old Covenant offered a way for God's people to minimally regain what was lost in the garden. They gained access to the living God through a high priest, but even he could enter into God's presence only once a year through the inner sanctuary of the tabernacle, the Holy of Holies. Both the requirement to access God through the Holy of Holies and the requisite process to do so reveals that such entry was not freely open. The high priest had to dress in specifically prepared, consecrated garments and present the appropriate sacrifice. He even tied rope around his waist, so he could be pulled out of the space in the event that he did not survive being in the presence of God.

Remember, God's will at creation was relationship and connection with His people. This intention remains, but the fall of man made necessary requirements to see that will accomplished. More was required—death. Just as the death of animals covered Adam and Eve and the death and blood of animal sacrifices atoned for the people's sin, death became necessary for God's will to be met.

Dig a little Deeper

READ HEBREWS 9:1-10.

What were the limits of the Old Covenant? What could it not do (v. 9)? _____

_____

_____

Why was the Old Covenant limited (v. 10)? _____

_____

_____

The Old Covenant was not designed to be a permanent solution. The high priest's sacrifices were imperfect and incomplete, but God had something better in mind than regulations of worship and requirements for good standing. He planned for more than the minimal access afforded by the covenant.

The Creator did not give up on His creation, though He had plenty of reason. Instead, He allowed the wilderness to be a place where He wooed the people with a better covenant and better promises. That new covenant would not be appreciated if the people had not experienced the wilderness; the old one barely allowed them to glimpse what God intended for them. It revealed to them their dire need for a Redeemer.

Refining Reflection

Exodus 25-31 lays out the requirements of the tabernacle, priests, offerings, and regulations of worship. Consider what living under the Old Covenant was like and offer thanks to the Lord that He had a better covenant to enact.

Additional Notes

_____

_____

_____

_____

_____

_____

_____

_____

Day 2

THE NEW COVENANT

L iving under the Old Covenant must have been overwhelming; it included so many regulations that affected one's good standing in God's will. It is no wonder Israel struggled. Her sin continually interrupted fellowship with God, yet He graciously provided a way for the people to regain fellowship through the system of sacrifices. This beautiful representation of the sinner's inner repentance and God's Divine forgiveness brought about the possibility of inheritance.

This week, we consider a will and will-maker. As we explore this concept, I want to bring clarity to the idea of the will from the perspective of God's being the Will-maker.

A will is a legal document, based on the will-maker's desires. Often when we speak of *God's will*, we understand it to mean *God's desire* for the believer. In Philippians 2:13, "the Greek word for *will* indicates that He is not focusing on mere desires or whimsical emotions but on the studied intent to fulfill a planned purpose."[10] Ultimately, this is His desire or determination for you. God's desire and determination for you is for His good pleasure—for you to do what satisfies Him. He is satisfied to call you His child and to bestow upon you the fullness of redemption, purification, protection, and inheritance that comes with being His child.

---

10 John MacArthur, "Note on Philippians 2:13," *The MacArthur Bible Commentary: Unleashing God's Truth, One Verse at a Time.* (Nashville: Nelson Reference & Electronic).

The term *will* in today's study of Hebrews is translated as "covenant"; however, the covenant that God establishes with us is directed by His desire and determination for us. As we forge ahead with the concept of the will as a legal document—a covenant—we must understand that it is a covenant created and directed by the Father's desire and determination for us.

Adam and Eve should have experienced physical death as a result of their sin, but God substituted an animal to foreshadow the reality that He would someday kill a Substitute to redeem sinners.[11] Death became the only way for His will to be enacted, but the death of animals at the hands of human high priests was incomplete and imperfect. A better covenant was needed to more completely satisfy the requirements already laid out in the will.

Consider the Context

Yesterday, we read in Hebrews about Old Covenant regulations that served as placeholders until a better system would be established. Today, we continue in Hebrews to consider the fullness of the New Covenant.

READ HEBREWS 9:11-14.

Which requirements from the Old Covenant did Jesus satisfy? _____

_____

What did Jesus' pure sacrifice have the power to do that the Old Covenant regulations did not? _____

_____

Jesus came as the perfect High Priest. He entered through the greater and more perfect tabernacle via His own perfect blood. He clearly fulfilled all requirements for the perfect Sacrifice, so why did many people reject Him?

---

11   MacArthur, "Genesis 3:21 Note," *The MacArthur Study Bible*. (La Habra: The Lockman Foundation), 21.

They expected Him to come in a blaze of glory, as a warrior king conquers an enemy in battle. While Jesus did just that, it did not look like what the people expected. They did not realize that death was still necessary to completely and perfectly enact the will of the Father.

READ HEBREWS 9:15-20.

What are the requirements for a will to take effect? _____

_____

Whenever my dad goes out of town on a trip, he reviews the location of anything in his house I might need, should something happen to him while he is away—particularly his last will and testament, which lays out my sister's and my inheritance upon his passing. His legal will takes what he *desires* me to have and puts it into a *covenant* that requires his death in order for it to be fulfilled.

I have a beautiful relationship with my earthly father. I treasure my time with him and value our connection, but the reality is that I cannot receive certain things until he passes away because the death of the will-maker is required for the legal covenant to be enacted. Only he can set the covenant in motion by meeting its requirement.

God's will—His desire—is that His children inherit the richness of His presence. If we consider the covenant He established to see that desire accomplished in terms of a legal document, we understand that the death of the Will-maker was required. Mankind needed a Priest and Sacrifice Who met the will's requirements once and for all, with no further need for repetition due to imperfection. Jesus Christ—God, the Will-maker in human form—is the only Person able to fulfill those requirements, and He offered Himself as the perfect High Priest and Sacrifice in order to validate and enact that covenant.

We established that today's passage translates the word *will* as "covenant." Consider that term as the same Greek word, translated as "testament"—as in last will and testament. The original Greek word takes on a more intentional meaning here because the benefits and provisions of a will are only promises until the writer of the will dies. Death, therefore, activates the promises and turns them into reality.[12] Thus, in order for us to receive the promises of God's testament, the death of Jesus Christ was necessary.

The provisions available through enacting the Father's will were infinitely better than that of the Mosaic Covenant, which offered only external provisions, keeping the inheritance as a promise to come but not a reality. The New Covenant, validated by Jesus' death, rendered the old one obsolete. "Then He said, 'Behold, I have come to do Your will.' He takes away the first in order to establish the second. By this will we have been sanctified through the offering of the body of Jesus Christ once for all" (Heb. 10:9-10).

The word *sanctify* means to make holy or to be set apart from sin. When Christ sanctified us, He made us holy and set us apart from sin for God. "When Christ fulfilled the will of God, He provided for the believer a continuing, permanent condition of holiness."[13]

Dig a little Deeper

READ HEBREWS 10:11-18.

How many times do you see the words *I will* in verses sixteen through eighteen? _____

Why is this significant? _____

_____

_____

_____

_____

12   Ibid, "Note on Hebrews 9:16-17," 1880.
13   Ibid, "Note on Hebrews 10:10," 1882.

The promises asserted in this passage remind us of the promise that was given to the Israelites in Jeremiah 31:31-34. At the time, it was an assurance of something to come, clearly stating that its fulfillment relied on God Himself and not on man.

READ HEBREWS 10:19-23.

How was the Old Covenant made obsolete? _____

_____

_____

Jesus' sacrifice was perfect; therefore, it was enough to cover all sins—past, present, and future. He perfected all who believe. Death is no longer required to atone. Rather, we must receive the forgiveness offered in the one Sacrifice Who covered it all. Through this forgiveness, we receive bold access to the throne of God!

The New Covenant moves us from external, earthly realities and to our inheritance in the presence of God. We no longer need the regulations of the high priest nor tabernacle sacrifices because the New Covenant cannot be broken. The sanctification Christ offers is permanent because His forgiveness is past, present, and future; it makes us acceptable before God. God's will for His people (His covenant with us, directed by His desire for us) to have access to Him and Him to them is enacted. The Old Covenant relied on the people to hold up their end of the bargain. The New Covenant relies only on our accepting the inheritance through the forgiveness offered by the death of the Will-maker.

Refining Reflection

How does the fullness of the New Covenant affect your identity? _____

_____

_____

How do your filters distort this new, sanctified identity in Christ? _____

_____

_____

The New Covenant gives us the position as children of God—a position held so deeply within the Father's heart that it cannot be lost, no matter our failure, inadequacy, nor fear. Our filters protest this position and create idols of obsession within our faults; but God, Who deems each one of us worth the price of the New Covenant, whispers to our hearts, saying, "You are enough; just come as you are."

Additional Notes

_____

_____

_____

_____

_____

_____

_____

_____

_____

_____

Day 3
A GLORIOUS INHERITANCE

The Old Covenant became obsolete when Jesus completely fulfilled its every requirement; with Christ, we are the heirs of the inheritance that released at that time. As heirs, we are given a vision of faith: the ability to see with the absolute assurance of God's perfect character and the truth of all He says, including what He says about us. Faith shapes our vision, as it is through faith that we become heirs. It is in our place as heirs and through this vision of faith that we can begin to recognize who we were created to be and why God woos us so diligently. It is in our identity as heirs that we accept and appreciate the will of the Creator.

Once the Law held us captive, preparing us for the greater covenant; now, faith draws us to Jesus Himself. Everyone who believes Jesus for salvation is now identified in the Father's will as the heir of a glorious inheritance. Sin caused us to lose the ability to hold the position originally created for us, and we became enslaved. Now we are not only set free but adopted. This adoption into the family of God drastically alters the identity in which the world cloaks us; yet it is the identity the Creator always intended.

When God created the path to adopt us, He did more than simply find a way to call us His own in a legal document; He provided a way to instill His very nature within us by giving us the gift of the Holy Spirit, who takes up residence in our hearts to transform and empower us. Being identified as an heir with Christ should awaken our sense of purpose and embolden our confident hope in Who God calls us to be.

Consider the Context

> But before faith came, we were kept in custody under the law, being shut up to the faith which was later to be revealed. Therefore the Law has become our tutor *to lead us* to Christ, so that we may be justified by faith. But now that faith has come, we are no longer under a tutor. For you are all sons of God through faith in Christ Jesus. For all of you who were baptized into Christ have clothed yourselves with Christ. There is neither Jew nor Greek, there is neither slave nor free man, there is neither male nor female; for you are all one in Christ Jesus. And if you belong to Christ, then you are Abraham's descendants, heirs according to promise. Now I say, as long as the heir is a child, he does not differ at all from a slave although he is owner of everything, but he is under guardians and managers until the date set by the father. So also we, while we were children, were held in bondage under the elemental things of the world. But when the fullness of time came, God sent forth His Son, born of a woman, born under the Law, so that He might redeem those who were under the Law, that we might receive the adoption as sons. Because you are sons, God has sent forth the Spirit of His Son into our hearts, crying, "Abba! Father!" Therefore you are no longer a slave, but a son; and if a son, then an heir through God (Gal. 3:23-4:7).

What major differences can you identify between our slavery and our position as heirs? _____

_____

_____

_____

What does receiving the Holy Spirit stir our hearts to cry? What does this tell us about the relational desire God has for us? _____

_____

_____

Faith is the vehicle through which we claim our identity as heirs and grow in understanding. We are no longer condemned but free to live in the will of the Father. We are rescued from the clutches of sin and death. Our title as heir grants us access to the Creator, a Heavenly Savior, a Heavenly calling, hope of an eternal future, and the honor of our own names' being written in Heaven. Once we wandered in darkness; now we have a place with a Father Who desires us and gives us the most precious thing we could hope for: direct access to Him.

This is our inheritance—Christ Himself in us—because everything the Father offers is possible only through Him. The same power that lives in Christ is in us. The same love the Father has for the Son is lavished on us. Sometimes, in the midst of our filters, we lose sight of the bigger picture—that we are called by the Creator Himself into a life of relationship with access to Him. When filters train our focus on the thing we do not have or a situation that does not seem to be going right, we miss the beautiful perspective of what He has done and desires for us. Flushing the filters brings the bigger picture into view, shrinking humanistic, subjective fears in the light of the riches of this glorious inheritance. "To whom God willed to make known what is the riches of the glory of this mystery among the Gentiles, which is Christ in you, the hope of glory" (Col. 1:27).

Dig a little Deeper

READ REVELATION 19:6-9.

Who is the Lamb, and who is the bride? _____

READ REVELATION 21:1-8.

When the Bridegroom claims His bride, what mutual benefit do they experience? _____

_____

_____

Remember, the will benefits both inheritor and will-maker. While we often focus on the beauty of our own gifts, it is easy to overlook another important factor—as we receive Christ, He, as the Son of God, receives His bride. We are His inheritance. That's right—we are the reward He deemed worthy of enduring leaving His Heavenly home, separation from His Father, and the torture of the cross. Our filters will trip us up in this reality and convince us that we are not good enough or have not done enough to deserve such riches. How could we be the inheritance that He so completely solidified?

These filters are wrong. They make us believe that claiming our inheritance depends upon our efforts to earn it; in truth, Christ's love for us cannot be dictated by our own actions. It is, in every way, determined by the Creator, Redeemer, and Will-maker. He underscored this truth by making and activating the New Covenant through His own perfect, complete sacrifice. Eliminating filters reveals that we are worthy simply because we are His handiwork. We are not a consolation prize that He settles for; we are the bride for whom He actively prepares.

Refining Reflection

Our vision of faith frees us to live in the knowledge and acceptance of this truth. It drives us to respond by basking in the love, wooing, redemption, and liberty of a God Who freely offers Himself as a better Covenant with promises that exceed anything we could achieve in our own flesh. I am so thankful for the fullness of the riches of His glorious inheritance in the saints.

How would your perspective change if you were to face any obstacles in your path with the big-picture knowledge we obtain in this inheritance? Commit today to intentionally considering the unfiltered glory of His inheritance in the face of our human struggles.

Additional Notes

_____

_____

_____

_____

_____

_____

_____

_____

_____

_____

_____

_____

_____

Week 6

# #

Day 1

THE SURPASSING GREATNESS
OF HIS POWER

A mundane rotation of farm duties and pitching in to make ends meet constituted the whole of Dorothy's life in Kansas until the day a tornado ripped through town and changed her perspective. Her house transported her and her dog to the magical land of Oz, where some of her filters shattered, revealing things about herself she never saw before. Suddenly, her grayscale vision transformed into a beautiful world of vibrant color.

On the journey that ensued, she found a courage she had been afraid to test, love she had been afraid to share, and wisdom she had previously left untapped. Had it not been for the monumental, nearly impossible task set before her, she never would have stepped into the identity she was meant for. At the end of road, the good witch Glenda shared some insight—the power had always been inside Dorothy; she had only to learn it for herself.[14]

We often find ourselves with grayscale vision; and like Dorothy, we need a transformation of vibrant color. Just as Dorothy awakened to the vivid land of Oz, it is time we awakened to "the surpassing greatness of His power toward us who believe" (Eph. 1:19). As we dive into the vibrant awakening, we discover the beauty that, as co-heirs with Christ, we have always had the power; we have only to learn it for ourselves.

---

14   *The Wizard of Oz*, directed by Victor Fleming (1939; Beverly Hills: Metro Goldwyn Mayer, 2005), DVD.

So far, we have closely examined Paul's prayer for the believer. Each piece is a building block for the next and culminates in this final appeal about the surpassing greatness of God's power. While we still have phrases of Paul's prayer to digest, this phrase gives the final ingredient for the life that is meant for the believer.

We discovered the need to simply ask for the spiritual wisdom that works and grows within the believer to develop our knowledge and understanding of Who God is and how He works. We recognize that our hearts, responsible for belief, need to be flooded with the light of God's presence in order to expose lies and brilliantly reflect our Creator.

As spiritual wisdom and knowledge of God increase, our hearts flood with light, embracing the identity meant for us and experiencing the confident hope of being called into the kingdom of God. Receiving our inheritance of Jesus and the Heavenly treasures that come with Him, while also being accepted and sought after as the inheritance of God Himself, further solidifies and confirms our identity in Him. This spiritual working, flooding, hoping, and identifying shatter the filters and expose the surpassing greatness of His power toward us who believe.

Consider the Context

READ EPHESIANS 1:19.

Consider at least three Bible translations (i.e., NASB, ESV, NLT). What other words are used for *surpassing*? _____

_____

How do these synonyms expand our understanding of the word? _____

_____

_____

What is this surpassing greatness of power? To surpass is to be immeasurable, absolute, and extraordinary. Other words—dynamic, energetic, might, strong—can be understood from the Greek terms Paul uses to describe God's power.[15] The word *surpassing* is a present participle that indicates the power is active. Not a past or future experience, it is present and ongoing. When used as an adjective of *greatness*, it speaks of a continuing, distinguished, respected quality.

It is important to recognize the gravity of pairing these words together. In describing God's power, they show a perpetual, actively immeasurable, distinguished force. Unmatched, it continually exceeds any other power.

This power spoke creation into existence. It brought forth light and gave darkness a boundary. It parted the Red Sea, provided manna for the Israelites in the wilderness, and raised Jesus from the dead. God's power and might are revealed to us through His marvelous works.

Dig a little Deeper

If you are at all familiar with the Bible, you have probably heard of the marvelous works of God. The best way to consider the reality of these works in action is to meditate on them in light of their perpetual, actively immeasurable, distinguished force. Once again, turn your focus away from your own abilities and focus on the unmatched power of God.

God's Power Over His Creation

Genesis 1:1-2:3 _____

_____

Exodus 3:1-2 _____

_____

---

15   David Jeremiah, "Note on Ephesians 1:19," in *The Jeremiah Study Bible: English Standard Version* (New York: Hachette Book Group, Inc., 2019).

Joshua 10:1-14 _____

_____

Luke 8:22-25 _____

_____

God's Power Over Death

John 11:1-44 _____

_____

Luke 23:44-24:12 _____

_____

God's Power Over His Enemies

Judges 7:12-22 _____

_____

Mark 5:1-13 _____

_____

Matthew 4:1-11 _____

_____

Refining Reflection

The active fullness of God's power leaves us speechless. The reality of
our Creator, Redeemer, and inheritance through Jesus crushes the filters of

fear and allows us to stand fully confident in His perfect power. Praise God for His unmatched power!

Consider times when you experienced the unmatched power of God: when, by all human understanding, things should not have worked out as they did. Maybe it was a moment of witnessing the power of His creation. Perhaps you saw God's power over your enemies or experienced the perfect peace in His power over death.

Reflect on those times and praise God for the surpassing greatness of His power. If you cannot recall a specific incident, ask Him to enlighten the eyes of your heart, so you may drop the grayscale vision and see His great power in vibrant color. We have only to ask.

Additional Notes

_____

_____

_____

_____

_____

_____

_____

_____

_____

_____

Day 2

POWER AWARENESS

The surpassing greatness of God's power knows no limits and has no equal. We could spend hours in God's Word, finding examples of His power; they will all show the same distinguished, active, extraordinary force. What we need to understand now is what Scripture means when this same power is extended "toward us who believe" (Eph. 1:19). Get ready for vibrant colors!

The identity of the believer is that of someone who believes God and puts action to that belief by making Him Lord and Savior of her life. Belief, in and of itself, is not enough. "You believe that God is one. You do well; the demons also believe, and shudder. But are you willing to recognize, you foolish fellow, that faith without works is useless? Was not Abraham our father justified by works when he offered up Isaac his son on the altar? You see that faith was working with his works, and as a result of the works, faith was perfected" (Jas. 2:19-22).

When we take the step of faith in accepting Christ as our Savior, we move past believing Who God is and accept Him as King. We deliberately repent of our sin and declare Him as Lord over all. This decision initiates a life of showing faith through works—not because salvation is tied to works (lest any of us think we can boast in our own capability)—rather, our works evidence the faith we declare.

This step of faith achieves the miraculous; we receive the surpassing greatness of God's power. The word *toward* is translated more clearly as *into*—the surpassing greatness of His power flows *into* us who believe. This word affirms an actual result and not a mere possibility.

God's power is given to every believer at the time of salvation. It raised Jesus from the dead and returned Him to His glorious seat at God's right hand and is always available to us. That is why Paul did not bother to ask that believers be given God's power; he prayed that they perceive the power already given to them in Christ and use it.[16]

Consider the Context

The power that raised Jesus from the grave lives in us. At the moment of salvation, when we are made co-heirs with Christ, we inherit the surpassing greatness of the power of God. In that moment, we are rescued from the domain, or the authority, of darkness (Col. 1:13). As co-heirs, we experience the same fullness that God the Father gives to God the Son—not a portion nor percentage but the wholeness of it.

The word *rescue* means to draw to oneself. When Christ rescued us from the authority of darkness, He drew us to Himself, covering us with His blood and extending His righteousness to us (2 Cor. 5:21). As a result, we are in Him. Since He has all authority over Heaven and earth (Matt. 28:18-19), we also have authority and power over darkness.

READ JOHN 14:16-17.

What is Jesus' request of the Father? _____

_____

Who is the Helper Jesus would send? _____

_____

---

16   MacArthur, "Ephesians 1:20 Note," *The MacArthur Study Bible*. (La Habra: The Lockman Foundation).

Where would He dwell? _____

_____

Jesus promised that when He was no longer physically present on earth, He would request that the Father send the Holy Spirit to dwell in believers. Indwelling occurred after Christ's ascension to Heaven. Believers had no need for the Spirit's presence before that, since both Son and Spirit are God Himself; therefore, God was already present in the form of the Son. Thus, God delivered on His promise to dwell in the believer when the Holy Spirit came upon them.

READ ACTS 1:8.

What would the apostles receive when the Holy Spirit came upon them? ____

_____

_____

The apostles had already experienced the saving power of the Holy Spirit, as well as His power in teaching, guiding, and working miracles. They were about to receive the indwelling of the Holy Spirit; this Presence is the powerful catalyst for the witness that spreads the Gospel to the uttermost parts of the earth. At the moment of salvation, we, too, receive the promised indwelling of the Holy Spirit. God's power within the believer is mighty, and all things become possible when met with the believer's obedience.

Dig a little Deeper

READ COLOSSIANS 1:29.

If God's power is working within Paul, how do you explain the word *striving* or *struggle* found here? _____

_____

We see Paul, *striving* in his labor for Christ, "according to His power, which mightily works within" (Col. 1:29). He serves and honors God with all his physical might, confident that the spiritual and eternal results are of God.

The power that "mightily works" within the believer is one that is energizing and effectually working, continually and actively. Note the word *striving*. "The Greek word for *striving* gives us the English word *agonize* and refers to the effort required to compete in an athletic event."[17] We cannot sit back and expect the Spirit to work mightily if we do not provide, through obedience, an avenue through which He can work. Our works must offer consistent evidence of our faith, perfecting it and giving way for the mighty working of God's power to be observed and experienced both inwardly and outwardly.

READ EPHESIANS 3:7.
God did His part in filling Paul with His mighty power. What was Paul's part?

_____

_____

"No man can make himself a minister (servant) of God, because the calling, message, work, and empowerment of genuine ministry to and for God are his prerogative alone to give."[18] Our calling into the kingdom of God makes us responsible to serve, manifesting of our belief and identity in Christ. "No one can serve two masters; for either he will hate the one and love the other, or he will be devoted to one and despise the other" (Matt. 6:24). We will either serve the darkness or serve the light. Since we have been rescued from the domain of darkness, we are called to serve the light.

What he *calls* us to do, he *enables* us to do through the power given to us at salvation (Heb. 13:20-21). Our gracious Lord knew the enemy would fight us on every step of this journey. Paul offers fresh perspective on the true power we

---

17   Ibid, "Note on Colossians 1:29," 1803.
18   Ibid, "Note on Ephesians 3:7," 1776.

possess in Ephesians 6:10. "Finally, be strong in the Lord and in the strength of His might."

Refining Reflection

Praying for access to this power is not necessary; we need only be aware and make use of it. What has God called you to do that requires obedience and leaning into the power He has already equipped you with? _____

_____

_____

_____

Additional Notes

_____

_____

_____

_____

_____

_____

_____

_____

_____

_____

_____

Day 3

GOD'S POWER IN ACTION

This week, I pray we grasp the beauty of God and the believer, working as one. The power of God, met with the believer's obedience, creates an incredible opportunity for the glory of the Lord to shine and flood hearts (not just our own) with the light of God's presence. A flooded heart can better experience the confident hope of being called into the kingdom of God and counted as an heir with and of Christ. It can work more effectively in the surpassing greatness of the power of God, which encourages spiritual wisdom and knowledge of God to grow. To others, it provides a living testament of the hope that awaits, if only they respond with surrender to the call.

As this week closes, let us soak in the reality of how God and the believer work together in harmony. On the first day of this week's lessons, we studied God's power over creation. Today, we return to Joshua 10:1-14 and discover not only God's power over creation but how it meets with His power within the believer.

The Israelites wandered the wilderness for forty years when God finally allowed them to enter the Promised Land. Taking possession of it was no easy task; they had to destroy all of the inhabitants of the land. But God began to give them victory.

In Jericho, the walls crashed down, allowing them to access the city and destroy the king. Turning toward Ai, they tasted defeat as a consequence of Achan's disobedience. Instead of following God's declaration that the spoils of Jericho belonged to Him and must be destroyed, Achan hid treasure for himself. Once the sin was exposed and punished in the valley of Achor (see Week 3, Day 3 of this study), Israel conquered Ai and hanged the king in a tree.

These accounts show what happens when God's people follow His Word. When the Israelites obeyed, God's power moved them to victory; when they did not, God's power still moved but as a reproach to their actions. Word of their conquests spread throughout the land, and kings feared. The power of God was evident, and His people were recognized as an extension of His power.

Consider the Context

Today's passage opens in Gibeon. Joshua 9 recounts that the people of the land recognize that, despite superior military power, they do not stand a chance against the Israelites and their God. Aware of God's instruction to destroy the land's inhabitants, they scheme to gain peace with Israel. Some of the men disguise themselves in worn-out clothes and load their donkeys with dried bread and cracked wineskins.

Approaching Joshua at Gilgal, they spin a tale of traveling from a faraway land in hopes of establishing a peace treaty to protect them from the wrath of the Israelites and their God. The leaders of Israel did not consult with the Lord before entering an oath with the men. When the truth emerged, that oath prevented Israel from harming the Gibeonites, whom they enslaved instead.

Gibeon, a great city with many mighty men, recognized the power of God through the Israelites so clearly and fully that they gladly became slaves to preserve their lives. The power of God sways hearts, minds, and actions, especially when met with the obedience of the believer.

READ JOSHUA 10:1-14.

Why did the five kings attack Gibeon? _____

_____

_____

Hearing that Gibeon made peace with Israel, five other kings conspire to join forces and attack Gibeon in an effort to keep Israel from adding strength and numbers to their fight. They fail to anticipate Israel's coming to Gibeon's aid. When Israel learns Gibeon is under attack, Joshua gathers his valiant warriors.

What command and promise does God give Joshua? (v. 8) _____

_____

_____

_____

What is Joshua's response? _____

_____

_____

_____

What evidence of God's power do you see in the battle that ensues? _____

_____

_____

_____

God had told Joshua not to fear and promised that not one enemy would stand against them. Obediently, the fighting men depart Gilgal and march all night, launching a surprise attack. God's power works once again; He confounds the enemy and slays them. Large hailstones fall from Heaven upon fleeing deserters and kill even more adversaries than the swords of the sons of Israel.

Dig a little Deeper

Imagine witnessing the surpassing greatness of God's power in action right before you. How might this have played a role in the prayer that Joshua prays in the midst of the battle (v. 12)? _____

_____

_____

_____

_____

_____

Joshua sees God delivering the Amorites into their hands. In the confident hope that God had given him, he calls out to the Lord in the midst of battle, "'O sun, stand still at Gibeon, And O moon in the valley of Aijalon'" (Josh. 10:12b). The sun stands still. The moon stops. For nearly a day, the sun stays high while the Israelites defeat the enemy.

Do not breeze past that fact. Pause to think about it. *The sun stood still.*

Joshua did not make this incredible request on a whim; his knowledge of God emboldened him to draw from confident hope in the power of God. In his place of obedience, he was able to do so because he knew God fought for Israel. Joshua's obedience and God's power worked in harmony. God heard His servant's request and made His glory unmistakably known to all who were there. Joshua's obedience, met with God's unmatched power, paved the way for the impossible to be made possible.

Philippians 4:13 says, "I can do all things through Him who strengthens me." We can have strength to withstand all things because God infuses us with His power at the moment of salvation—"the surpassing greatness of His power toward us who believe" (Eph. 1:19).

Refining Reflection

Surely, the Lord fought for Israel that day. As our knowledge of God grows, we understand that His heart for Israel reflects His heart for His people. As co-heirs, we can expect, hope for, and tap into the power of God. It is already there, and we need only obey to fulfill our role in this partnership.

Where might your obedience, met with the power of God, change the tide of battle and pave the way for the impossible to come to fruition? _____

_____

_____

_____

Additional Notes

_____

_____

_____

_____

_____

_____

_____

_____

_____

Week 7

Day 1

THE STRENGTH OF HIS MIGHT

For several weeks, we have examined what Paul desires for the believer; today, we concentrate on the bookends of our prayer. God, and only God— the Creator of all things—can impart to us spiritual wisdom, knowledge of God, hope, inheritance, and power. We ask "the God of our Lord Jesus Christ, the Father of glory" (Eph. 1:17) for the richness of each of these treasures, and we know we can ask in confidence "in accordance with the working of the strength of His might" (Eph. 1:19).

My youngest child anticipated her sixth birthday like only a first grader can. She talked about it for weeks. She thought carefully about what presents she wanted for her birthday, what kind of party and—of utmost importance— the cake.

When she finally decided on the cake she wanted, she knew who to ask. Mommy has always been able to make her cake dreams come true. She approached me without stopping to question if I was able to do it, if I thought I could make it work, or even if I had seen anything like it before. No, she confidently put in her request for unicorn donut cakes because she believes in my ability, based on the proof of past experience. Once she asked, she did not worry about it; she waited, expectant.

On the day of her birthday party, she squealed dramatically with excitement at the result: a tower of multicolored donut cakes, covered with unicorn sprinkles over purple and pink icing and topped with a sparkling horn. It was magical, just as she believed it would be.

Asking with confidence means we actively look for the result of our petition. It is possible when we know who we are asking, combined with the power they have to provide the outcome. That power is trustworthy because of who holds it and the proof of past experience.

Paul knows Who he is asking—the God of our Lord Jesus Christ, the Father of glory. He links the Father and the Son in Deity, acknowledging that They share the same essence because the Trinity of God points us toward His power. He trusts the power because of Who God is.

My daughter trusted my cake-making ability because of what she had already seen and experienced, and she had the confidence to ask me because she knows who I am. Her experience was not that of a bystander but as a child intimately connected to the love, nurturing, and discipline of my character as her mother. If we gloss over the bookends of Paul's prayer, we miss the gravity of knowing the character of our God and the confidence it imparts in making expectant petitions.

Throughout our study, we have reflected on Who God is, His attributes. We recognized the Creator's majesty and the Father's love. We soaked in the light of His glory and humbled ourselves in the awe of His grace. The better we know God's character, the closer we draw to Him, knowing we can bring our petitions to Him because of Who He is.

Consider the Context

Once mankind needed a human mediator to approach the Father; through Jesus, we can go to Him directly. Understanding our position in Christ and knowing God's heart toward us allows us to do so with confidence.

Consider what each of the following passages teaches us about God and man.

Ephesians 3:12

What do I learn about God? _____

_____

What do I learn about man? _____

_____

Hebrews 4:15-16

What do I learn about God? _____

_____

What do I learn about man? _____

_____

James 4:8

What do I learn about God? _____

_____

What do I learn about man? _____

_____

Hebrews 10:19-23

What do I learn about God? _____

_____

What do I learn about man? _____

_____

1 John 3:22

What do I learn about God? _____

_____

What do I learn about man? _____

_____

John 16:22-24

What do I learn about God? _____

_____

What do I learn about man? _____

_____

Matthew 7:7-8

What do I learn about God? _____

_____

What do I learn about man? _____

_____

Ephesians 3:20

What do I learn about God? _____

_____

What do I learn about man? _____

_____

Each time the Scriptures encourage us to approach the throne boldly or to simply ask for what we need, we are reminded of who we are in light of God's grace and Who He is in His power and promise. Making these requests reminds us of our need for Him to intervene on our behalf while reinforcing our identity in Him as His children.

Paul begins his prayer, focusing on Whom he petitions. He makes his request known and reminds us of the evidence of the power that makes it possible. Closing the prayer with "in accordance with the working of the strength of His might" (Eph. 1:19), he recognizes God's power and ability and points to the evidence of Christ's rising from the dead. Pay attention to "the working" of the strength of His might. Once again, we notice that working, continual, active nature of His strength that is translated from the Greek as energizing and effectually working. The *Who* is God in the fullness of the Trinity; the *power* is evidenced in all He has done. We see the evidence of creation all around us, and the resurrection of Jesus establishes God's power even more clearly.

Dig a little Deeper

READ ROMANS 1:1-5, PAYING CLOSE ATTENTION TO VERSES FOUR AND FIVE.

How is each member of the Trinity active in these verses? _____

_____

What power is displayed by each member of the Trinity and by the Trinity as a whole? _____

_____

Jesus Christ is declared the Son of God (His place in the Trinity) by the evidence of the resurrection. Let us consider this concept of declaring by painting a picture. The Greek root of our English word *horizon* actually means "to distinguish." The horizon marks a clear line between earth and sky. Christ's resurrection makes a distinction, as well, by establishing a clear line between humanity and Deity. The resurrection clearly distinguishes Jesus

Christ as Deity with irrefutable evidence that He is the Son of God, a title we often take for granted with regular use. This title identifies Jesus' essence and God's as being the same; therefore, it is "unquestionably the expression of God Himself in human form."[19]

The resurrection, Jesus' victory over death, undeniably shows Jesus' place in the Trinity as the Son of God. It also gives credence to the role of the Holy Spirit, Who gave direction and power to the Son as He submitted Himself to the will of the Father. All three Persons of the Trinity worked together to reveal to mankind the truth of *Who* He is and the *power* He possesses.

Revisit the following passages from last week. This time, consider not only the power of God but also His heart behind the power.

Luke 8:22-25

His power: _____

His heart:_____

John 11:33-34

His power: _____

His heart: _____

Mark 5:1-13

His power: _____

His heart: _____

We believe in the power of God because of Who He is; we gain our confidence from the evidence of the power displayed. I love to hold on to this

---

19   Ibid., 1658.

quote by Victor Raymond Edman in moments of uncertainty: "Don't doubt in the darkness what you knew in the light."

As we set down the path of growing in spiritual wisdom and the knowledge of God, the enemy will try to detour us. He does not want us to love God more, nor does he want us to realize the hope and power within us. He wants to blind us with filters that trap and distract, and doubt is one of his most valuable resources. Make no mistake—he will use it. In times when that deceptive little seed of doubt is planted, we must return to what we knew in the light.

The glory of the Creator's light flushes filters, revealing Who He is and who we are. His light reveals truth and gives the darkness a boundary. When the enemy tries to surround you with darkness, hold tight to what God's majestic presence already revealed to you. Seek the Light Himself—the *Who*— to disrupt the darkness. Do not allow the filters to make you doubt what you knew in the flooded heart. Then allow Truth to rush over you as you remember the evidence of His power—the evidence of the resurrection, of creation all around you, and what He has done in your situation.

The bookends of Paul's prayer remind us that no matter how caught up we might get on the details of what we are asking, *Who* we are asking is infinitely more important. The strength of His might energizes us as it works, showing us how He works on behalf of the believer.

Refining Reflection

Take time today to reflect on the evidence of God's work in your own life. How has He shown Himself and His power to you specifically? Perhaps He opened a door, blessing you beyond imagination. Maybe He closed one to protect you from a path He knew was not good for you. In moments of darkness, when doubt threatens our resolve, remember how the God of our Lord Jesus Christ, the Father of Glory, already showed you His presence and power.

THE BEGINNING AND THE END

John 1:1 tells us, "In the beginning was the Word, and the Word was with God, and the Word was God." And we read in Revelation 22:13, "'The Alpha and Omega, Beginning and the End'"—everything starts and ends with Him, and everything in between is because of Him. As we continue to study the bookends of Paul's prayer, we see that this theme goes far beyond his prayer for the believer and is found throughout the entirety of God's Word. It points us to Him, not us—to His power, not our own.

Our filters try to bring us to the forefront of the picture, making us think everything is about us and how we fit into the bigger picture. I can tell you this for sure—one of the fastest and surest ways to shatter a filter is to return focus to the Alpha and Omega. We fade into nothingness in the light of the great I Am.

As we realize that He is far above all rule, authority, power, dominion, and every name that is named in this age and the one to come, we find ourselves on our knees before Him, rather than bowing to our own filtered idols. Everything starts and ends with Him, and everything in between is meant to glorify Him.

Have you ever noticed that when we ask the Lord for something, our focus can easily get stuck on that one thing? Even praying for spiritual wisdom, which is meant to draw us into a deeper awareness and understanding of Him, can lead us to playing the measuring game. We have such a knack for making things about us that we begin to try to compare the spiritual wisdom we think we have gained against how much we think we should have. We even rate ourselves among people around us to determine whether we have more spiritual wisdom than they do.

Do not say you have never done it; we all have. Saying it out loud makes it sound ridiculous, though, so we do not want to admit it. When I speak about spiritual wisdom aloud, it is apparent that I have missed the point of needing and praying for spiritual wisdom altogether. Contemplate asking the Lord to make you a good wife and mother. Maybe you have come to an awareness that He called you to those roles, and you want to honor Him. You also recognize your husband's need for a wife who helps him achieve the Lord's calling for him. You see your children's need to grow in the nurture and admonition of the Lord and your great responsibility in accomplishing that. Your request is born of an awareness of who you are and your desire to honor the Father.

But soon, as you pray for Him to make you a good wife and mother, you begin comparing yourself to other women around you. You decide you have to improve because Sally Jo is better than you, or you need to excel in that other area because you do not meet Jane's expectations. What started as an honorable request between you and the Father becomes a self-focused, self-measured endeavor. Your motives are no longer rooted in honoring the Father.

Consider the Context

As your focus shifts from Him to you, your motives become tied to the measuring stick you hold. It is a stick that measures you against people around you, rather than God's Word and heart for you. You have begun to allow warring passions within you to get what you want through your own devices and introduced a foothold for a filter. You get frustrated when you do not see the answer to prayer you hoped for. You try harder to be the mom who has it all together and the trophy wife who looks good on your husband's arm. The original intent of your request shifts focus. Filters have slid into place; now you ask for something good but with the wrong reasons.

READ JAMES 4:1-7.

What do you learn about man in these verses? _____

_____

_____

How does trying to a trophy wife and supermom reflect the way a love for the world supersedes love for God? _____

_____

_____

"Whoever wishes to be a friend of the world makes himself an enemy of God" (v. 4). How can we request to be a good wife and mother while maintaining friendship with God and distance from worldly pursuits? _____

_____

_____

"You ask and do not receive, because you ask with wrong motives, so that you may spend it on your pleasures" (Jas. 4:3). Saying, "Help me be a good mom, so everyone will think I have it all together," sounds superficial and ridiculous. Is this not what our hearts, left to their own devices, lean to? "The heart is more deceitful than all else And desperately sick" (Jer. 17:9).

We must give ourselves the bookend mentality to consistently check our focus. Am I still focused on God, or am I caught in the weeds? The bookend mentality brings me back to the reality of my own inability and wicked heart and turns me back to Jesus, lest I boast in anything of my own making. Everything starts and ends with Jesus. When I keep these bookends properly in place, I am less apt to get caught in the weeds and more likely to experience the fullness of what He has for me.

Dig a little Deeper

O Lord, our Lord, How majestic is Your name in all the earth,

Who have displayed Your splendor above the heavens!

From the mouth of infants and nursing babes You have established strength

Because of Your adversaries,

To make the enemy and the revengeful cease.

When I consider Your heavens, the work of Your fingers,

The moon and the stars, which You have ordained;

What is man that You take thought of him,

And the son of man that You care for him?

Yet You have made him a little lower than God,

And You crown him with glory and majesty!

You make him to rule over the works of Your hands;

You have put all things under his feet, All sheep and oxen,

And also the beasts of the field, The birds of the heavens and the fish of the sea,

Whatever passes through the paths of the seas.

O Lord, our Lord, How majestic is Your name in all the earth! (Ps. 8).

David penned this beautiful psalm of praise, revealing the beautiful result of bookend mentality. His opening address, "O Lord," identifies God's specially revealed name, Yahweh, followed by "our Lord," addressing His sovereignty. David starts with Who God is and the power He possesses, encompassing the fullness of God.

How does starting this Psalm by focusing on the fullness of God drive the rest of the passage? _____

_____

When we start with Jesus, a mental shift occurs that brings us out of the confines of our own understanding and reveals the vast expanse of possibilities that await us. It changes how we see things. As David continues, he does not get distracted with the workings of the heavens and the earth themselves but observes how they declare the splendor of Yahweh. He experiences the beauty of creation as an expression of God's majesty, seeing that everything—even the mouths of infants—testifies of His strength and silences His enemies. In the light of Yahweh, the enemy has no power.

We were created as an expression of God's majesty. Though we are mere mortals, God is mindful of us and has bestowed upon us what three things (vv. 4-5)? _____

_____

We are creations who are cared for by the Creator and given position near Him. At the moment of our salvation, we receive the power of God. In light of this, how should we stand before our enemies? _____

_____

Do you see the power that awakens in us when we realize that no enemy stands a chance in light of Yahweh? The same power that lives in us silences the enemy, rendering him powerless. The first bookend introduces us to flooded hearts and minds, where we actively look and confidently expect the splendor of our King.

In verse three, David's worship of God's splendor and strength expands to include humans, mere mortals. It remains within the context of the Creator and acknowledges that we are nothing, yet God Himself is mindful of us. Again, all things regarding man are first put in perspective of Yahweh. We see that, although man is nothing in light of Yahweh, it is Yahweh Himself Who gave us a crown and made us who we are. We view ourselves in light of what the Creator has made of us and how we can display His splendor. This type of mindfulness challenges thoughts that shift our focus onto ourselves and fixes the view of ourselves firmly in the light of Yahweh—all that we do and have are by Him and for Him. This knowledge points us back to "O Lord, our Lord, how majestic is your name in all the earth" (v. 1).

Filters do not belong anywhere near God's creation. They distort, distract, disregard, and destroy what God created us to be and do. They stop us from fulfilling our purpose of glorifying the Father. When we live in a bookend mentality, recognizing that everything starts and ends with Jesus, our entire perspective in between becomes Jesus.

Our filters remove us from the context of Yahweh and into a place where deceitful, wicked hearts can roam unchecked through a life of measuring sticks and frustration. Consistently starting with and returning to Jesus brings our thoughts, experiences, and identity to Jesus. Filters are recognized faster and destroyed more fully because they are not Jesus. May we live, breathe, and move in the state of *always Jesus*.

Refining Reflection

Would you say your life could be defined as *always Jesus*? How would your thoughts, experiences, and identity change if you adapted the bookend mentality? _____

_____

_____

_____

_____

_____

Day 3
ALL TO JESUS

"I Surrender All" has always been one of my favorite hymns, with its sweet melody and powerful words. Growing up in the Baptist church, I sang this song often. I probably knew it by heart by the time I was five. As I got older, I began to consider the words more closely. Do I surrender every last bit to Jesus?

It is easy to say we surrender our trials to Him—we have come to our end and realize that only He is able to deliver us. Surrendering is simpler when we feel the situation is out of our hands, anyway. What about things that are firmly grasped within our control? My desires feel like they are within my control. I want chocolate; I eat chocolate. Do I freely give Him even my chocolate? The act seems so minimal, insignificant. Does He *really* want my chocolate? Friends, He really does.

For some of you, that truth might be a deal-breaker—you are ready to toss this entire study in the garbage because now we have crossed a line. Why in the world would He want your chocolate? What could it possibly do for Him? The answer is that it is not the chocolate He cares about. He cares about the complete surrender it took for you to give it to Him.

Living an *always Jesus* life means even the smallest, most insignificant things pale in comparison to the love and trust you have in Him. The desire to live in His presence with flooded hearts greatly overwhelms the need for the worldly treasures.

Sometimes, we find ourselves in a quandary. Which comes first, the desire to live an *always Jesus* life or surrendering the things that keep you from it?

Do we not have to desire it if we are going to surrender to it? Do we not have to surrender to it, in order to taste it, so we can desire it?

We could spend hours in circular thinking; instead of wasting that time, know that wherever you are at this moment is exactly where you need to be to surrender. Hand over the chocolate—yes, even the chocolate. If you cannot manage to offer Him the small things, how can you expect to hand over the bigger ones? How can you surrender filters if parts of you are unwilling to give over to the Creator to be developed as He sees fit?

Consider the Context

READ ROMANS 12:1-2.

What is Paul's appeal for physical surrender in verse one? _____

_____

What does he mean by this? _____

_____

What is Paul's appeal for a surrender of the mind in verse two? _____

_____

What does he mean by this? _____

_____

What is Paul's appeal for surrender of the spirit in verse two? _____

_____

What does he mean by this? _____

_____

Paul draws upon the wellness trifecta, calling for surrender of body, mind, and spirit. These elements are responsible for everything in our lives, encompassing the physical health of our bodies, the mental wholeness of our minds and thought patterns, and the spiritual strength of our connection and relationship to the Father. We are called to surrender the trifecta: presenting our bodies to serve when, where, and how God calls; yielding our minds to the transformation God has for us; and giving ourselves over to the discernment of the Holy Spirit's moving within us.

When we consider an *always Jesus* mentality, we must be prepared to surrender all: body, mind, and spirit. We cannot hold on to one while surrendering the others; eventually, the one we grasp will wither and, rather than being supported by the other two, be the cause of their destruction. We must stop conforming to the world and begin transforming to the image of Christ.

To conform to something is to don a mask and blend into the picture or expectation around us. Transformation is a change that originates inside, forming the image-bearer we were created to be. That change comes only with total surrender. Our only acceptable workship is offering ourselves completely to the Lord.

Our bookend mentality of *Jesus first, Jesus last, always Jesus* makes us aware that where there is *always Jesus*, there is no room for me.

You may be thinking, *Wait, Jodi. You have told me this entire time that I am a treasure, a creation who needs no filter, and that I need to step into the life God has for me. How can you now say there is no room for* me *in all of that?*

You *are* a treasure and a creation who needs no filter. You do need to step into the life God has for you. In order to experience the fullness of that, we must let it all go—the insecurities that made room for filters and the control to which we cling. Let Jesus move instead. Release fear and trust the Savior. Drop those little things you might be tempted to think are insignificant and show Jesus you treasure nothing more than Him.

Does this surrender mean He will never let you have chocolate again? No, instead of hoarding it to eat in secret, you will enjoy it infinitely more when He is the One to give it to you.

Dig a little Deeper

READ THE FOLLOWING PASSAGES AND NOTE WHAT AN *ALWAYS JESUS* IDENTITY LOOKS LIKE.

Galatians 2:20 _____

_____

_____

Romans 6:1-6 _____

_____

_____

2 Corinthians 5:15-17 _____

_____

_____

"I have been crucified with Christ; and it is no longer I who live, but Christ lives in me; and the life which I now live in the flesh I live by faith in the Son of God, who loved me and gave Himself up for me" (Gal. 2:20).

The *always Jesus* bookend mentality shows me that as a believer who lives with the hope of His calling, "it is no longer I who live, but Christ" in me. No room exists for me because the old me is gone. I am a new creation, being made into the likeness of Jesus. This true identity is what I am meant to reflect, but I must surrender to it. I must be willing to continually, actively consider myself as nothing and Christ as everything.

This thought process differs significantly from what filters encourage. Filters say I am nothing and must always strive harder to achieve value. In an *always Jesus* life, the idea that I am nothing is actually a relief. Accepting that my worth is not questioned nor determined by what I can offer in my own strength is a joyous thought. Jesus deems me worthy. He made me new and is the reason I have hope. I gladly surrender everything because Jesus is Life, the Light of the world, the Victor over darkness.

Refining Reflection

What is your chocolate? What "insignificant" things do you need to surrender to Him to show you treasure nothing more than Him? _____

_____

_____

_____

Is your wellness trifecta completely surrendered to Jesus? Where might you need to focus your surrender more intentionally? _____

_____

_____

_____

Where have you struggled with earning your own worth? What would it look like to step back and rest in the truth that your worth is neither questioned nor determined by what you do to earn it? _____

_____

_____

_____

Additional Notes

_____

_____

_____

_____

_____

_____

_____

_____

_____

_____

_____

_____

_____

_____

_____

_____

_____

_____

_____

Week 8

Day 1

A WORTHY WALK

What a beautiful journey we have experienced so far! For the past seven weeks, we confronted filters, challenged lies, and flooded our hearts with light. We opened the door to a new life while we step in confident hope as Christ-followers, owning the brilliance of who we are in the eyes of the Creator Himself.

On this faith journey, we have begun to discover the vision that is meant for us—one that clearly reflects the power of the risen Savior within us and the Father's love that chases us, transforming our wilderness into flowing rivers. We claimed a long-awaited identity that awakens who we were meant to be with Jesus at the beginning, end, and in between.

We laid aside burdens of self-imposed expectations, reveling in the truth that we do not have to prove our value to be found worthy because the Creator already declared it. We felt the great relief of realizing that this filter-free life has nothing to do with us and everything to do with Jesus.

We sat in deep humility as truth saturated our hearts; even in my mess, He loves and wants me, and He proved it on a cross. We are called out of darkness to salvation and life in the light of Jesus. It is such an enormous honor to be called out of my filth to be loved, honored, and considered a precious inheritance of Jesus. The knowledge should leave you speechless and overwhelmed but firm in who it *makes* you because of Who *made* you.

As you step into this beautiful calling with flooded hearts full of hope and power, you must do one thing: "Walk in a manner worthy of the calling with which you have been called" (Eph. 4:1).

Does a princess walk around in yesterday's workout clothes and a week-old, messy bun? (If you answered *yes* to that, we need to talk.) No, a princess does not go out looking like a hot mess, even if she feels like one. She walks in a manner that is worthy of her title and position.

We have the title "Daughter of the King," and our position requires a proper walk. Now, we do not need to take princess classes or know when to bow to whom or the correct table setting to dine with dignitaries. Our training concentrates on three areas—position, posture, and apparel. Today, we consider our position.

Consider the Context

The key to understanding and owning our position in Christ is remembering who you **are** versus who you *were*. This concept is clearly defined by *Whose* you are and *whose* you were.

READ EPHESIANS 2:1-3.

Describe *who* you were before Christ. _____

_____

_____

Describe *whose* you were before Christ. _____

_____

_____

Who we were and whose we were before Christ prevented us from having a relationship with God. We were deceived by the enemy, blind to our true condition, unfit for a holy God, and living for our own selfish desires. Before Christ, we were dead. We existed in a world that operates by its own sense of humanity, values, and standards that are desperately far away from God. It is a domain of darkness, where the prince of the air, the enemy, rules with malice. His goal is to steal, kill, and destroy. He ensnares you with the lusts of your flesh and leads you to indulge the desires of your flesh and mind. This domain of filters, lies, deceit, and sorrow kept us captive.

We must remember what we were and where we came from if we are to hold our new position in a manner worthy of the calling—to acknowledge that before Christ we were nothing, lost, and without hope. *But God . . .*

Dig a little Deeper

READ EPHESIANS 2:4-9.

What did God do to make us His? _____

_____

_____

How did God's mercy and love change our position from who and whose we were? _____

_____

_____

What was our condition in the midst of God's action (v. 5)? _____

_____

_____

In His rich mercy and steadfast love, God calls us out of that dark domain and lavishes upon us an identity of worth. His grace covers multitudes of sin and shortcomings. My being called out of this darkness has nothing to do with me *on purpose.* In His infinite wisdom, God knows I need to recognize both the depth of my inability and the limitless nature of His power and grace; at no point along my journey can I think I had any part in my exodus from the darkness. It is all by His grace through faith. My only role is to believe and, in that belief, to receive His grace.

We were nothing—helpless, powerless, slaves to sin. We belonged to the darkness. But now, we belong to a risen Savior, a merciful and gracious Creator Who loves us and gave Himself for us. He paid the debt that bound us in darkness and brought us into the light, not as slaves but heirs. We are new creatures with new names; a new position of honor, blessing, and grace is bestowed upon us. Who we *were* is gone. The darkness holds no power over us. Who we *are* is rooted firmly in the Creator Who loves, chases, and transforms us into someone of worth.

If we are to walk in a manner worthy of this beautiful calling, we must destroy filters that tell us we are not enough and rest in the truth that Jesus has made us enough. He deems us worthy, and He defeated death to prove it to us. He is the reigning King, God Almighty, Alpha and Omega; if He deems me worthy, nothing in this world can change that—not even my filters.

Refining Reflection

Examine the filters that distort the view of your position as an heir with Christ. What gives them power—your insecurities or fears? Surrender them to the Father today. Choose to own your position as daughter of the King. Owning your position makes you ready for posture. _____

_____

_____

_____

Day 2
OUR POSTURE

Owning our position requires that we accept the Creator truly does love us that much. In our heads, we know what He did for us; we truly step into our position when we accept everything He says about us, rejecting anything else. Once we accomplish that, we are ready for the *posture* portion of our training. This idea is so much easier to discuss than to actually accomplish. When doubts threaten to overshadow the light, keep the *always Jesus* life in mind: surrender doubt, fear, and disbelief to Him. Owning our position is a constant, continual choice, as is maintaining the posture it requires.

When I was a teenager, my parents constantly told me to stand up straight. It always reminded me to be mindful—not just of how I held myself in that moment but also how I carried myself. Our conduct represents who we are. Our posture should reflect our position. If my position is that of royalty, my posture should show me worthy of that position. My walk must demonstrate behavior that matches my position in Christ. Yesterday, we considered the significance of who and whose we are. This concept establishes our position. Knowing one's position is one thing; remembering it is another.

Every time I drop my kids off at an event with their peers, I say, "Remember who you are and whose you are!" The intentionality of remembering our position shapes how we reflect it. I want my children to keep in mind the integrity of who they are and the Creator to Whom they answer; so they are mindful of their actions, words, and thoughts when their mama is not present to hold their hands through it. Setting that deliberate priority supports an active posture that accurately reflects their identity in Christ, and its purpose is twofold: they walk in confidence, and others see an accurate reflection of the Creator's love and power.

Consider the Context

READ EPHESIANS 4:1-3.

What five things describe a posture that is worthy of the calling? _____

_____

_____

_____

Humility

Humility requires a difficult balance. I have known people with false humility, fear disguised as humility, no humility, or self-deprecating humility. The humility Paul refers to here is a balanced awareness of who we are and Who God is. It is the most foundational virtue for any Christian.

How does God's response differ between pride and humility in James 4:6? __

_____

_____

_____

The first character quality described in the Beatitudes depicts a humility that is deeply rooted by the recognition of our hopelessness apart from God (Matt. 5:3). Most importantly, it is the attitude of Christ Himself that we should emulate.

> Do nothing from selfishness or empty conceit, but with humility of mind regard one another as more important than yourselves; do not merely look out for your own personal interests, but also for the interests of others. Have this attitude in yourselves which was also in Christ Jesus, who, although He existed in the form of God, did not regard equality with God a thing to be grasped, but emptied Himself, taking the form of a bond-servant, and being made in the likeness of men. Being found in appearance as a man, He humbled Himself by becoming obedient to the point of death, even death on a cross (Phil. 2:3-8).

Never confuse humility with weakness. Our Lord Himself was the very definition of true humility. This is lived out by considering others as more important than yourself because the moment you think you are better or more valuable than anyone else, you lose sight of the foundation of your position. You were *nothing*, made to be *something* by the Creator. Never forget that.

This truth holds beauty and confidence. We can be confident and humble at the same time because we are secure in the One Who gives us our position but humble enough to realize that we did nothing to earn it. This truth informs how we view others, recognizing that we are simply saved by grace in the same way that God saved them or wants to save them.

We are to be confident in humility, a concept so foreign to the world in Paul's time that no word existed in the Latin or Greek then. The Greek word for humility was apparently coined by Christians, perhaps Paul himself, to describe this necessary quality.[20] We should look different because we do not fit within the world's standards of conduct; instead, we imitate Christ.

Gentleness

Gentleness is properly placed next in our lineup because it is an inevitable product of humility. Gentleness, or meekness, is the outward manifestation of our inward humility and reflects an ability to practice self-control. The

---

20 Ibid, "Note on Ephesians 4:2," 1777.

opposite of weakness, gentleness is actually strength that is kept under control. It turns away wrath with a soft answer (Prov. 15:1), even when the flesh begs to issue a tongue-lashing.

Gentleness puts the idea of considering others as more important than yourself into action. It forgives a wrong instead of retaliating. It promotes an environment of rest, emulating our gentle, humble Lord, Who gives rest to the weary (Matt. 11:29). It is a fruit of the Spirit (Gal. 5:23) and a characteristic of the new man (Col. 3:12). As the Spirit transforms us into Christ's likeness, our life reflects His character.

Sometimes, when our humility wavers, gentleness can bring us back in line. Although I may not feel like giving a soft answer, the intentional (if difficult) choice to do so awakens the spirit of humility and helps me reset. While indulging the temptation to allow emotion to drive our responses can be so much easier, gentleness is the wise choice to control how we answer, guiding outward action to realign with appropriate humility.

Patience

If we could skip this one, I would. Patience tests you like nothing else, but it is a continued result and outward showing of our humility and gentleness. The inner heart of humility, reflected in the outward show of gentleness, gives growth to long-tempered patience. Impatience stems from an unwillingness to wait because our time is more important. Lack of patience often stems from pride or a lack of self-control—exactly what must be brought under control through humility and gentleness.

It makes sense that patience is an outgrowth of these traits. They are all tied together; when one them suffers, they all do. But when we return to the foundation of considering others more important than ourselves, we respond kindly and compassionately, with a Spirit-led ability to wait on God's timing in our lives and in others' lives. Humility is the reality that it is not about me; gentleness is the action that shows it; patience is the long-tempered proof of it.

Tolerant love

As you can see, each one of these posture pieces builds on the last, and tolerant love is no different. Showing tolerance for one another in love is a culmination of the behaviors. Tolerance here is the same as forbearing. *Merriam-Webster* defines forbearing as "holding back or abstaining; to control oneself when provoked."[21] Please do not miss this point—putting forbearance into practice is not easy. The concept of forbearing shows us that our flesh still finds things wrong with other people. Even when we approach true humility, gentleness, and patience, we still have conflicts with other people. We are flesh. Our humility, gentleness, and patience will be tested; but they will also have opportunity to be reflected in a forbearing love for others.

Love must be part of the equation; without it, we are left to our own devices to hold back and keep our mouths shut whenever we feel wronged or slighted. Love gives that frustration an avenue to be worked out. I choose to hold back in forbearance and to love the person who wronged me. Loving her means I remember to consider her more important than myself. I consider her needs without holding her sin against her. "Above all, keep fervent in your love for one another, because love covers a multitude of sins" (1 Pet. 4:8).

Showing tolerant love does not mean becoming a doormat and allowing others to stomp all over you. At times, you may need to walk away from toxic people in your life but not with anger, malice, or bitterness. We remove ourselves, so we can continue to lift them up in prayer for the Father to tend to them. If we stay around those toxic people, we are far more likely to begin acting like them, slowly losing the posture that is worthy of our position. Be fervent in our love for one another.

Being fervent means remaining intensely passionate, even when circumstances stretch you to the limit. A runner races with everything she has. Her muscles' output reaches maximum capacity, yet she continues, passionately

---

21   *Merriam-Webster*, s.v. "forbear," accessed December 4, 2023, https://www.merriam-webster.com/dictionary/forbear.

intent on reaching the finish line. Stretching yourself to the limit in fervent love requires you to put another's spiritual good ahead of your own desires, no matter how that person treats you. Maybe she is unkind, ungracious, or even hostile toward you. Being fervent in love helps you look past the poor treatment to see the heart of her spiritual need.[22] No poor behavior gives you license to assume any posture other than what is worthy of your position. It is not easy, but it is a choice. No ill treatment gives us license to act in any way other than with the posture that is worthy of our position. It is not easy, but it is a choice.

Diligent Preservation of Unity

A bond of peace exists between each believer. It is created as the Spirit develops a oneness among the body of Christ and holds us together in unity that we must be diligent to preserve. Once again, this state is easier and more naturally accomplished as a result of our worthy posture.

Through humility, gentleness, patience, and tolerant love, we are in a prime position to build each other up, respect each other's talents and efforts, and admonish one another to carry good posture. We assume a supportive role that is comfortable enough in our confident humility to take a back seat, if necessary, while someone else has the opportunity to shine for the glory of God. As women, this means we must stop viewing each other as competition.

Read that again. *We must stop viewing each other as competition.*

In our family, everything is a contest. My husband and I tease each other at the end of each day about who beat whom in our fitness tracking goals. He always beats me, by far, and it used to discourage me. I felt that my accomplishment was not as significant. I realized there is no need for that. I am happy when he doubles his daily goals, but I have barely reached mine. My goals look different than his for a reason. He did not carry and deliver four children and undergo three surgeries in a ten-year period. He just has to think about losing a few pounds; losing a few of pounds requires my blood, sweat, and tears.

---

22   MacArthur, "Note on I Peter 4:8" (2006).

A little competition can be fun and motivating; however, it can become a snare to unity and peace all too quickly when motives take on the face of pride. Insecurities allow filters to distort the competitor. Diligently preserving unity among believers means that humility checks our pride. We remember that all of us are working toward the same goal. When a sister in Christ achieves the goal, I do not need to be irritated that she got there first because the Father was glorified when she reached it. It is our shared goal. Therefore, I rejoice with my brothers and sisters when they do great things for the Father. I admonish, encourage, and continue working with them toward the goal of glorifying the Father by walking with a posture worthy of my position.

Dig a little Deeper

As each of these posture pieces grows stronger and more intentional, our back straightens; our shoulders slide back; and our heads poise to balance the crown that comes with being a daughter of the King. Our posture is put into motion. It is in no way a posture of pride or arrogance but of confident humility. We can now walk in a manner worthy of the calling, for this posture allows us to walk in love, light, and wisdom.

READ EPHESIANS 5:1-5.

How do we walk in love? _____

_____

_____

As imitators of God, we are to love as He loved. A love that imitates God's can have no impurity nor selfish motives because it is not self-serving; rather, it is patient and kind. This love requires the attitude of humility that was in Christ, considering others more important than ourselves. Immorality cannot exist in this love. It is the pit in which filters flourish and self-control, gentleness, and patience get lost. In order to keep filters from flourishing, we must be others-focused, not self-consumed.

READ EPHESIANS 5:6-14.

How do we walk in light? _____

_____

_____

Empty words create filters. Rooted in darkness, they stir up trouble. You have been rescued from the darkness. You are a resident of the light now and have the power to expose empty words with the light. Nothing is exempt from being affected by light. No filter is too firmly placed nor lie too deeply believed that cannot be rooted out by exposure to light.

The best way to expose these things to the light is to keep yourself exposed to the Light. Continue flooding your heart and flushing the filters. Continue soaking in God's Word and allowing it to transform you to be more like Him.

Humility positions us to receive the light. Gentleness allows us to use the light. Patience allows us to wait on the light. Tolerant love allows us to take a back seat to the light. Diligent preservation of unity allows us to shine the light. Pursuing these postures is how we *walk* in the light.

READ EPHESIANS 5:15-21.

How do we walk in wisdom? _____

_____

_____

As believers, we must be aware of what happens around us. We need to observe and acknowledge the players in the room and, mindful of the Lord's will, we must walk appropriately. Walking in wisdom leaves no room for anything that controls your senses nor invites habits that are unfitting for the position you hold.

When Paul speaks of not being drunk with wine, he specifically refers to pagan worship ceremonies of the day that were excuses to conduct drunken orgies in the name of whatever god suited at the time. These events were believed to create supernatural, enthusiastic communion with the gods. Thankfully, God does not require such horrifying, drunken escapades. True communion with God is not introduced through drunkenness at all but by the Holy Spirit. Paul's admonition not to be drunk with wine precedes a command that charges believers to live continually under the influence of the Spirit. We accomplish this goal by consistently taking in the Word of God, allowing it to direct our outlook, pursuits, and interactions with one another.

Being filled with the Spirit means living in constant awareness of Jesus' presence—letting His mind and Word dominate every thought, word, and action. Being filled with the Spirit cannot be separated from walking in the Spirit, as they are one and the same.[23]

Walking in wisdom means every thought, word, and step come back to Jesus—*Always Jesus*. Our posture pieces—humility, gentleness, patience, tolerant love, diligent preservation of unity—work together to help us walk and talk in a way that is fitting and worthy of our calling. Walking in love, light, and wisdom yields the elegant posture that becomes us and reflects the Creator Himself.

Refining Reflection

Where does your posture need work? Will you surrender today to intentionally walk with a posture that is worthy of your position? _____

_____

_____

_____

23   Ibid, "Note on Ephesians 5:18," 1782.

Day 3
OUR APPAREL

We acknowledge our *position* by remembering who and Whose we are. We remember the worthy posture required for our position. Today, as we prepare to say goodbye to our filters once and for all, we focus on dressing the part.

If we are truly a rags-to-riches story, it is time we toss the rags and don apparel that is fitting for our position and posture. Our position is one of royalty, so we must be prepared to dine with the King and ready to defend against enemy threats. Our apparel should reflect elegant strength and gracious dignity. "Strength and dignity are her clothing, And she smiles at the future" (Prov. 31:25).

It is fitting that we clothe our position of confident humility in strength and dignity. This strength draws from the confident hope and power we have in Christ; dignity comes from a genuine execution of a humble heart. Our apparel's strength calls on our confidence, allowing us to do battle with the enemy at any moment; however, it is not so overstated that we appear prideful, as if it had anything to do with us. It is refined armor, fashioned by the King Himself and worthy of the position He gives us. We put it on with a permanence that testifies no other apparel will do.

Consider the Context

READ EPHESIANS 6:14-17.

List the pieces of our appropriate apparel:

1. _____

2. _____

3. _____

4. _____

5. _____

6. _____

Walking in the victory of flooded hearts and destroying our filters requires an interwoven effort of our position, posture, and apparel. The way they work together forms the very fabric of how the Creator intends us to live—the finished surface that reflects our true colors as His redeemed creation. Let us don our apparel, one vital piece at a time.

The Belt

A belt holds up clothing or supports what it surrounds. It can also carry objects like tools and weapons. In addition, it defines or accentuates the waist. A staple piece in a woman's ensemble, it is often used to tie everything together.

A proper belt has the potential to make the entire outfit, but not just any belt will do for a daughter of the King. Ours is a belt of truth, fashioned from the Light-giver Himself. Its purpose is threefold: to keep our trousers in place, to carry our tools and weapons, and to accentuate the beauty of the Creator.

First, we work on keeping our trousers in place because—let us be honest—no good comes from falling trousers. Have you ever worn a pair of pants that are just a bit too big? Without a belt, they are unreliable and quite a nuisance. You spend all day, tugging them back into place or risking unwelcomed exposure if you fail to catch them in time. If one hand is engaged in preserving my dignity, I have only one left to use in the task before me. My mental focus splits between the pants and the task I need to accomplish.

In Roman times, a soldier wore a loose-fitting tunic. Can you imagine a warrior in battle, fretting about his tunic's whipping in the wind or catching on his weapon? Obviously, this dilemma proves disastrous in hand-to-hand combat. Not only could the flapping clothing hinder movement, but it could also distract his focus to the point of costing his life. Cinching up that excess fabric was of grave importance.

Paul's mention of girding our loins refers to a soldier's process of securing loose ends in preparation for battle. To his point, truth represents the belt that pulls in spiritual loose ends. Girding our loins with the belt of truth—a deliberate act of self-discipline—tucks away everything that hinders us, so we commit to fight and win without hypocrisy.[24] Our belt needs to hold our trousers in place and tie up any loose end that could distract us or feed the filters. The belt of truth allows us to focus on our commitment to our position and posture because we do not worry about loose ends to cause problems. Filters create loose ends; the belt of truth binds them and eliminates power over your position and posture.

Our trousers secured, we now have a place to carry tools and weapons. Our tools of trust in the Savior, hope in His calling, and exposing light are securely fastened to our belt of truth. Their anchor in truth lends strength that makes them more likely for us to grab during the mission. They also have the unique flexibility of becoming our weapons when faced with enemy forces.

We operate and speak in truth. In so doing, we achieve the trifecta: trousers up, weapons fastened, the Creator accentuated. The truth of who and Whose we are accentuates the beauty of the Creator Himself, as we reflect the position and posture that is worthy of our calling. Our belt of truth causes all eyes to turn to Him and all glory and worship to go to Him.

---

24   Ibid, "Note on Ephesians 6:14," 1784.

The Breastplate

Any set of armor needs a piece that protects the soldier's torso, home of vital organs. The breastplate has taken on many shapes and sizes throughout history, but its purpose is protecting the soldier from wounds that could cause irreversible damage. It must be tough and resistant to enemy attacks, which is why we don a breastplate fashioned from the righteousness of God Himself.

When Jesus imputes His righteousness to us at the moment of salvation, we inherit protection from the enemy's schemes. Living faithfully and obediently in communion with the Father enacts that protection. This continual exposure to His righteousness knits together our breastplate. We grow to understand how His integrity and virtue protect our hearts. Without integrity, virtue, and Christ's justification, our hearts are left exposed to the enemy; the fight will be over before we realize it began. The breastplate of righteousness affords us a position of integrity and posture of virtue—not because we are good but because we reflect our exposure to the Light.

The Right Pair of Shoes

Marilyn Monroe once said, "Give a girl the right shoes, and she can conquer the world."[25] Sadly, I do not believe that Ms. Monroe had any idea of the depth of truth in this statement. The shoes of the Gospel of peace empower and embolden. Ready for any terrain, they are classy and worthy of our position.

These shoes are not the type that *look* good but, put to the test, require every ounce of self-control not to wince in pain with each step. You know the shoes I mean—those adorable heels that stay in the back of the closet because they are just too cute, but you never wear them because they are also the most impractical contraption your feet ever wore. The shoes that constitute our

---

25   "Marilyn Monroe Quotes." n.d. Brainy Quote. https://www.brainyquote.com/quotes/marilyn_monroe_498600. Accessed February 19, 2024.

proper apparel ground us in the solid truth that believers are at peace with God. It is the foundation from which all confidence grows, allowing us to stand firmly rooted, regardless of the ground we navigate.

We have all experienced a shoe mishap at some point. I once picked the wrong pair for an occasion and found myself ill-prepared for the terrain. Instead of being properly grounded, my feet led to wherever comfort or security could be found. Unfortunately, that situation may not lead me where I need to be. Our proper shoes resemble the Roman soldier's—boots with nails to grip the ground and ensure secure footing in combat. We need secure footing on the path of walking worthy of our calling.

Our adversary tries desperately to filter our vision with lies that question who we are and where we stand in the eyes of the Creator. The Gospel of peace gives us security by rooting us in the Truth that we are at peace with God, and He is on our side. This knowledge enables us to stand firm in confidence and frees us to claim His promise to be our strength.[26] The right pair of shoes gives movement to the surpassing greatness of God's power in us who believe. With His power awakened in us, feeding our confidence, we can conquer the world because darkness gives way to the light every single time.

The Shield

"For by grace you have been saved through faith" (Eph. 2:8). Faith is complete, absolute confidence and trust in God. Faith believes that all He says and does is true and right. Putting on the shield of faith levels up our apparel game exponentially. The belt of truth secures loose ends; the breastplate of righteousness allows brilliant light reflection; the right shoes plant us firmly in the reality of an unquestioned relationship and peace with God. The shield of faith protects us from enemy fire. The enemy will attack our position, but the shield of faith blocks him and reveals the lie.

---

26 MacArthur, "Note on Ephesians 6:15," 1784.

Attack: You have no value.

Shield: I have been bought with a price.

Attack: You are nothing.

Shield: I am loved, honored, and called by name.

Filters cannot be placed if they are never accepted. It is our faith—our continual trust in God and His Word—that protects us from taking on these filters, these arrows. The shield of faith keeps our posture upright because it gives darkness no opportunity to flourish.

The Helmet

Salvation is God's most treasured, secure gift to the believer, and we don it as our head covering. As a crown declares the status of the wearer, our helmet shows our status as heirs with Christ. The head was a major target in battle; our minds are a major target for the enemy. When you think something long enough, your heart begins to believe it. What your heart believes gets pumped through your veins and has the ability to become life-giving or toxic. Attacks on the mind are constant and unrelenting. Doubt and discouragement can grow like a cancer, eroding our posture and leaving us unable to walk worthy of our position. The security of our salvation in Christ is the only thing strong enough to protect against the doubt and discouragement that are sure to be fired at us.

Our salvation brings confident hope that reminds us of who and Whose we are. The security of our identity as a daughter of the King is worn as protection for the mind to keep us focused in the right place, rather than distracted by filtered images of distorted identities.

The Sword

This piece fastens firmly to the belt of truth, and the light of God's Word emblazons its hilt and blade. It is used both offensively and in defense. It is the truth of Scripture—the most powerful weapon that exists and the only one we need.

Our position gives us the right to wield this powerful weapon. Our posture helps us know how to wield it. We must practice with this weapon daily, knowing every inch of its blade and detail of its hilt. We must know the weight of it as we lift it high and the motion of it as we move through battle. With it, we will see victory, protect all other apparel, and hold our position firmly in a posture that is worthy of a daughter of the King.

Refining Reflection

Position secure, posture appropriate, and apparel donned, we do not shy away from battle but stand ready to fight. We are ready to charge ahead. We know Whose power is within us, enabling our position, supporting our posture, and fashioning our apparel. We trust Him for every piece of it, and we will live in a manner worthy of our calling. Filters have no place here. May we choose to live free of filters and worthy of our calling.

Apparel Check

Does your belt hold up your trousers, or are you running around with only one hand available? Why? _____

_____

_____

_____

Does your integrity brilliantly reflect the Creator? Why or why not? _____

_____

_____

_____

Are you running around in shoes that make you wince, or have you grabbed the right pair? Why or why not? _____

_____

_____

What does your shield look like? Does it need work? How can you use it to its full potential? _____

_____

_____

What toxic beliefs does your helmet of salvation need to destroy? _____

_____

_____

Has your practice with the sword prepared you for battle? Why or why not? _

_____

_____

Additional Notes

_____

_____

_____

_____

_____

_____

ONE FINAL THOUGHT

Filters are meant to distort the original view. It is my hope and prayer that as we have walked together through exposing the filters and replacing them with God's Truth, you find confidence that you, God's creation, need no filter. Let us stop defining our worth by the measurement of a lost world and turn instead to the Creator Himself. Flood the darkness with His light. Flush the lies that deplete your confidence. Stand firmly in the hope of His calling, the riches of His glorious inheritance, and the surpassing greatness of His power that dwells within you as a child of God.

Let us make no more excuses for self-doubt and fear. Walk in a manner worthy of your calling and see God take the spotlight and move mightily to crush the filters. Be prepared to unleash who you were created to be for the glory of the Almighty.

In today's world of social media, the hashtag is used to identify ourselves or the content we share, enabling others to find and possibly identify with it, as well. Your identity and value are securely rooted in the One Who created you. As we step into our calling with the position, posture, and apparel of royalty, may we identify ourselves and the content of our lives as having #nofilter. Let it be an identifier that draws the attention of others who desperately need to shatter imprisoning filters and find rest in the truth of God's grace.

Praise God, we need #nofilter.

BIBLIOGRAPHY

Brainy Quote, n.d. "Marilyn Monroe Quotes." Accessed February 19, 2024. https://www.brainyquote.com/quotes/marilyn_monroe_498600.

Craver, Ben. "Hope." *The Lexham Bible Dictionary*. Ed. John D. Barry et al. Bellingham: Lexham Press, 2016.

Henry, Matthew and Thomas Scott. *Matthew Henry's Concise Commentary*. Oak Harbor: Logos Research Systems, 1997.

Jamieson, Robert. *Commentary, Critical and Explanatory on the Whole Bible*. Grand Rapids: Zondervan Publishing House, 1997.

MacArthur, John. *The MacArthur Bible Commentary: Unleashing God's Truth, One Verse at a Time*. Nelson Reference & Electronic.

Merriam-Webster. S.v. "forbear." Accessed December 4, 2023. https://www.merriam-webster.com/dictionary/forbear.

Odor, Judith A. "Light and Darkness." *The Lexham Bible Dictionary*. Ed. John D. Barry et al. Bellingham: Lexham Press, 2016.

ABOUT THE AUTHOR

Jodi Hendricks is a wife and mother of four beautiful children. A native of Albuquerque, New Mexico, she attended Bob Jones University in South Carolina, where she graduated with a bachelor's degree in creative writing and a master's in interpretative speech.

She moved back to New Mexico with her husband, Michael, in 2007 and later earned a master's degree in counseling from Wayland Baptist University. Jodi practiced as a licensed mental health counselor for several years, serving women who struggled through depression, anxiety, and mood cycling disorders.

In 2021, she became the executive director of New Mexico Family Action Movement (NMFAM), where she works to create, advocate, and defend public policy that protects biblical values.

Jodi loves to study and teach the Word of God. As an author, speaker, and the founder of *#crowned* Ministries, she shares unique perspectives from Scripture to teach women valuable, life-changing truth.

Contact Information

www.hashtagcrowned.com

Ambassador International's mission is to magnify the Lord Jesus Christ and promote His Gospel through the written word.

We believe through the publication of Christian literature, Jesus Christ and His Word will be exalted, believers will be strengthened in their walk with Him, and the lost will be directed to Jesus Christ as the only way of salvation.

For more information about AMBASSADOR INTERNATIONAL please visit:

www.ambassador-international.com
@AmbassadorIntl
www.facebook.com/AmbassadorIntl

Thank you for reading this book!

You make it possible for us to fulfill our mission, and we are grateful for your partnership.

To help further our mission, please consider leaving us a review on your social media, favorite retailer's website, Goodreads or Bookbub, or our website, and check out some of the books on the following page!

MORE FROM AMBASSADOR INTERNATIONAL

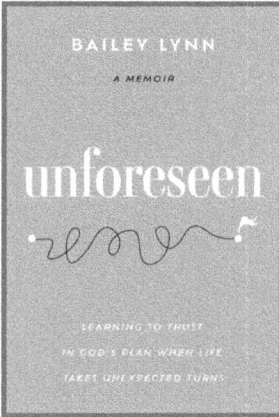

Bailey Lynn had her life perfectly planned. She thought she was on the path God had preordained for her. But when her life took an unexpected turn, Bailey was left to question God's ability to dictate her life. In *Unforeseen: Learning to Trust in God's Plan When Life Takes Unexpected Turns*, Bailey shares how she learned to trust God with a future she had never planned. As she battled whether God's plans for her were truly as good as He had promised in His Word, Bailey began to see His ways were definitely not like hers—they were better.

When Kathy Vintson finds herself upside down with her underwear on full display at, she suddenly realizes just how chaotic the world can be, and she is reminded of the Crown Effect—that she is a daughter of the King, Whose unmerited favor is to love her, even when her granny panties are on full display. Using humor and humility as her guide, Kathy takes a deeper look into what it means to be truly loved by the King of kings and how to bask in His love and peace, even when the world feels like it is closing in.

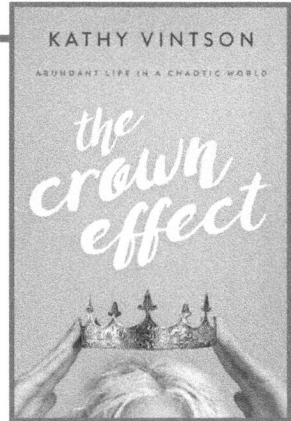

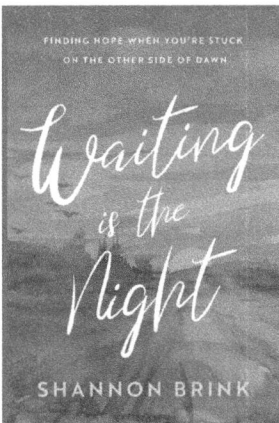

We all go through seasons of waiting, times when God just seems to have closed His ears to us and turned His back. During those seasons, it's easy to give up hope and lose heart. What can we learn from those times of waiting? Drawing from her own experiences and from the examples of God's people in the Bible who also experienced seasons of waiting, Shannon encourages the reader to hold on to the One Who created us. While waiting in the dark, cling to the Light.

www.ingramcontent.com/pod-product-compliance
Lightning Source LLC
Chambersburg PA
CBHW071436090426
42737CB00011B/1675